Other Works by Farley Dunn

Relentless Love

How God's Unshakable Devotion
Can Change Everything

*Experience the Depth, Power,
and Purpose of the Love that
Never Lets Go*

Relentless Love

How God's Unshakable Devotion
Can Change Everything

———— *Farley Dunn* ————

RELENTLESS LOVE: HOW GOD'S UNSHAKABLE DEVOTION CAN CHANGE
EVERYTHING

By Farley Dunn

1st ed.

Subtitle: EXPERIENCE THE DEPTH, POWER, AND PURPOSE OF THE LOVE THAT
NEVER LETS GO

Contents

Introduction

The Love of God.

In the church, we have many terms for it. Agape Love. Divine Love. Brotherly Love. Even Christ's Love for Humanity.

Christian theology offers us even more insight with terms such as Unconditional Love, Preferential Love, and Supernatural Love.

The truth is that all of these are correct yet none of them tell the whole of how much God loves us.

How many of us would suffer the most horrific of deaths by *dying of suffocation on a Roman cross?* Even for someone we love, it's an immense ask of dedication and devotion.

So, let's lay some ground rules to help us understand what we mean when we talk about the Love of God.

Agape Love is selfless and unconditional—the love God has for us and expects us to have for our fellow man.

Divine Love flows from God's supernatural and transcendent nature. We see it described in the New Testament.

Philia or Brotherly Love is how we reveal the Love of Christ with our fellow Christians.

Christ's Love is revealed through his teachings and sacrifice and is meant to inspire us to love others.

Unconditional Love is a gift independent of our actions or the conditions of who we are.

Preferential Love is Christ's example of extending love especially to those most in need.

Supernatural Love emphasizes the divine nature of Christ that transforms the believer rather than a natural emotion that comes easily to us.

So, whether you say God's favor, saintliness, piety, holiness, virtue, or sanctity, know this: God's Love is a life-changing force that will create a new you, one that will be empowered to change the world for the better. Invite Christ in. He wants to make a difference in your life.

— I —

Love That Never Fails

The Unbreakable Nature
of God's Love

*Give thanks to the Lord, for He is good; His
love endures forever.*

— Psalm 136:1 —

Unbreakable!

What does that mean to you? What things in life
do you think of as unbreakable? I want us to talk
about physical things for a moment, things we can
reach out and touch. They will give us a concrete,

understandable Rosetta stone for everything else we look at in this chapter.

So, what do you imagine as unbreakable in your home, your city, your place of employment? Another way to picture this is what is the most durable substance you can use in an application if money is no issue?

Stainless steel? We use it for sinks, industrial kitchens, and anywhere that rust cannot be allowed.

Stone? In the Northeast, it's often used for curbing or door stoops. We face our houses with it and top our kitchen cabinets with it. It's difficult to damage or stain.

Laminated glass? It is close to unbreakable, the reason we find it in car windshields, high-rise windows, and even in use as structural walls or flooring.

What do these concepts reveal? Things that are considered unbreakable are best used in stressful situations to withstand the worst that life can throw at us. Stainless steel, stone, and laminated glass all serve different purposes; but we place our trust in them because they are the best items we have for the applications for which we use them.

The same is true of God's Love. When we are

broken, lost, or in need of protection, we can depend on him.

Before Time Began

I have loved you with an everlasting love ...

— Jeremiah 31:3 —

Everlasting love ... that sounds pretty unbreakable to me. And the word everlasting goes both ways, into the past and the future. Look at God's provision of a perfect home for Adam and Eve. He provided for all their needs, including companionship of both the mortal and divine. He also provided them with responsibility and a purpose, that of caring for his creation, including the naming of the animals.

An even stronger example is Abraham and Isaac. It's in Genesis 22:1 where the word love first appears in the holy text. "Take your son, your only son Isaac, whom you love ..." Then God makes Abraham choose between God and Isaac. The depth of God's love for Abraham is revealed when the angel stays Abraham's hand at the moment of his sacrifice and reveals the ram caught in the bushes.

God provided the sacrifice he requires. All he required was that Abraham place his trust fully in the Lord so that God could step in and bring Abraham's faith into full and tangible reality. Abraham believed that God could—and would—provide, whatever the form and process that God's provision might entail.

The first epistle of John sums up the love of God in three words: "God is love ..." (I Jn 4:16). There is nothing God can do that falls outside of his love. It is in his nature, in the very concept of who he is, how he operates, and how he interacts with his creation. And that means with us, his children.

The eternal nature of God's love is revealed in John 17:24: "You loved me before the creation of the world." This is Jesus speaking, but the intensity of the relationship between the Father and his Son is unmistakable. There is a bond of trust revealed in Jesus' prayer, one that can only come through a level of love that is eternal and unbreakable.

There are more examples of God's love permeating the Bible. We've read the story of Caleb and Joshua, whom God honors because they place their trust in him. Job ... what a love we see in the story of

Job when God says to the devil, "His life you may not take." There's David who reveals the love of God through his collection of psalms.

And we can't forget Mary, the virgin that Joseph thought to put aside. God stepped in and made her the honored one who would forever be seen as the mother of the Christ.

Finally, though, let's look at the supreme example of God's eternal and unbreakable love. You've already seen it in Mary's story and in the archetype of the sacrificial lamb as revealed through the story of Isaac. God loves his creation so much that when his plan for his chosen people stumbled, he pulled out a backup plan from off the shelf, one he hoped wouldn't be necessary, but one he accepted as vital to redeem those who could not redeem themselves.

He sent his Son to live among his creation, to learn to be human, to experience the highs and lows of living with his feet on the ground amid the bickering and often cruel people who claimed to worship God and yet quarreled about the reality of God's existence. God sent his Son to suffer the worst fate the Roman world could offer, a slow and agonizing death of suffocation while in the most extreme pain possible.

Could you do the same? This was a father who had loved his son (in Jesus' words) "before the creation of the world." This was a relationship so concrete, so stainless steel, so laminated glass that it was unbreakable ... a bond of love stronger than superglue and more indestructible than stone.

God released Jesus to be born as a baby in a world gone mad ... and Jesus agreed to take on the challenge. That's love, one that began even before the clocks of time existed.

Love that Pursues the Lost

Doesn't he leave the ninety-nine ... and go
after the lost sheep?

— Luke 15:4 —

Redemptive love ... a level of love that refuses to break the chain of commitment that bonds people together. This is another type of unbreakable love, an ingrained element of God's nature, one that not even he can ignore or shunt aside.

This verse in Luke harks back to a time that's

unfamiliar to modern society, that of animal husbandry as a way of life rather than a weekend hobby. The Savior in this example is compared to a shepherd, an occupation whose job description includes total protection for every member of the group. A good shepherd strives for a one-hundred-percent survival rate for his flock; and for each animal to receive a level of care and protection that makes them feel secure against any threat or accident that befalls them.

The Good Shepherd. That's Our Lord and is intrinsic to the nature of God from the beginning of time. He's the laminated glass that refuses to give way even when we stumble and crash against the barrier of his love, a wall that, in our distress and self-destruction, seems to not be there.

The Children of Israel received God's redemptive love when he released them from the bondage of captivity in Egypt. What had begun as a place of security for the Israelites, offering protection from a famine that threatened to subsume all the land with starvation and death, became an inescapable cage of brutality and slavery. Through the leadership of Moses, God led his people out of Egypt and established the Mosaic Covenant with the Israelites.

We love the story of the Prodigal Son found in Luke 15:11-32. The son squanders his inheritance, and still, the father holds his arms wide to embrace his wayward son upon his return. This heartfelt example of redemptive love showcases how God receives his creation when they return unto him.

Job's story underlines how faith and restoration work in God's plan. When we place unwavering faith in God's redemptive power, God will draw us in and offer us greater blessings than we had before our troubles began.

As children, we heard the story of Jonah over and over. Even the secular world has popularized the iconic tale of spending three nights in the belly of the fish. Yet, we mustn't miss the vital core of the narrative, the true meaning the Bible wants to get across to us. God so desired to offer redemption to the city of Ninevah that he used a giant fish to change Jonah's mind and bring him to repentance, so that he would preach God's forgiveness to Ninevah, which led to the conversion of the entire city.

And we can't forget Paul ... or perhaps we should name him Saul, a man instrumental in persecuting the early Christians. When the biblical story of Saul/Paul opens, the man is a deadly opponent to those who have placed their trust in the Christ. He is the worst of the worst, searching out those in the newly formed Christian sect, and calmly observing as they are brutalized and even killed *at Saul/Paul's hand.* In Acts 7:58, as Stephen was being stoned, the Bible tells us that "the witnesses laid their coats at the feet of a young man named Saul." Yes, this is the same Saul/Paul who is the author of many of the most revered books of the New Testament. Yet—and this is important—God's love affair with mankind was so unbreakable that he dramatically transformed Saul/Paul on the road to Damascus, and a newly renamed Paul went on to become a leading apostle and evangelist … and the author of much of the New Testament.

God does the same for us. We were lost, and in his redemptive love, we are restored to wholeness through the sacrifice of Jesus on the cross. It is his death and resurrection that atone for our sins and offer us eternal life and a relationship with God. Even in times of profound loss or sin, God's love pursues us so that we might know his redemptive nature. His love offers us hope and encouragement that can transform even our most broken lives and relationships.

Unchanging in a Changing World

I the Lord do not change ...

— Malachi 3:6 —

The nature of the world around us is rooted in change. An easy example is found in the seasons of the year. Life erupts from the soil in spring, then rolls into the heat of summer. We enjoy the brilliance of fall foliage and bundle up as winter's blast rattles the windows in our homes. Then, the cycle begins again.

Change. The ever-evolving cycle of the seasons. What we see out our window now is impermanent, only for today. We've heard the old saying that if we don't like the weather, wait five minutes. It's bound to change. Yet, even in the changing weather and seasons, we can find stability and security. When storms thunder and rain darkens the afternoon, clear skies will return. When winter blankets the land, the green shoots of spring will indeed break through, the trees will bud with leaves, and the days will lengthen and bring summer's warmth once again.

The immutability of God's unchanging nature means that his essence, character, and purpose never change. He consistently fulfills his promises. Isaiah 40:8 tells us that the grass withers and the flowers fall, but the word of our God endures forever. His love for us doesn't waver no matter what we've done. His justice and righteousness consistently align with his written words, and his wisdom, goodness, and holiness are revealed in each of his actions and in what he requires of his people.

Most importantly, God's grace is offered to us as a gift. We never have to earn it, and it cannot be lost. God is at work in our lives, and he guides our footsteps into new paths, but HE does not and cannot change. Our children will grow and leave the home; our years of employment will one day come to an end; our place of residence will change from this city to that; but during our seasons of change, God's unbreakable love never changes.

Abraham's story is a perfect illustration of God's unchanging nature and love. He is called to leave his home, and God promises to make of him a great nation. God makes a covenant with Abraham that his descendants will become as the stars, and they will inherit the lands of Canaan. When Abraham fathers Isaac, Abraham's unwavering obedience invokes God's unchanging love, and God provides a ram—instead of Isaac—for a sacrifice. Abraham's legacy of obedience, faith, and trust in God is solidified by the unchanging nature of God as revealed by God's fulfillment of his promises to Abraham.

We also see this in the biblical narrative of Jesus and his temptation. After being baptized by John the Baptist, Jesus enters the desert where he fasts for forty days in preparation for his ministry. During his time of preparation, the devil tries to knock Jesus off God's ordained path of ministry and eventual sacrifice with three temptations.

First, Jesus is tempted to eat. After forty days of hunger, this seems like a no-brainer, at least according to Satan. "Eat, feast, just turn the stones on the ground into sweet bread. You deserve this treat." Isn't that sometimes like us? We feel like we *deserve* what the devil holds out to us. Jesus stands on the unchanging love of the Father and says, "Man does not live by bread alone but by the word of the Lord."

Satan takes another approach and appeals to Jesus' connection with his Father. He says, "Jump from the temple. Angels will catch you, for God will never allow any harm to come to you." Jesus replies, "Do not put the Lord your God to the test." God didn't have anything to prove. Jesus had confidence that the Father loved him. His trust in God's promises was rock-solid.

Finally, the evil one promises Jesus power and glory. He shows him the kingdoms of this world and suggests that they can belong to Jesus if he will switch his allegiance from God to him. Jesus rebuffs him, saying, "Back down, Satan. God is the only one I will worship and serve."

The story of the temptations of Jesus demonstrates how the unchanging love of God helps us to overcome in every situation. It highlights the nature of Jesus as the Messiah, the Son of God who will bring redemption to mankind. It is a model for Christians on how to overcome temptation and underscores the ongoing battle between good and evil—between God and Satan—and illustrates specific examples of how to resist temptation and live a life pleasing to God.

The world may change but God never does. His love is the same yesterday, today, and forever.

No Strings Attached

While we were still sinners, Christ died for us.

— Romans 5:8 —

We love the idea of getting something for free, but most "freebies" aren't really free at all. We trade our time and resources for the "free" veggies we grow in our backyard garden. That "free" healthcare is covered by taxes or premiums. Even the "free" repairs under warranty programs are covered by the higher prices manufacturers charge for their products.

This title of this section is "No Strings Attached." Imagine getting a birthday gift and being told that it's yours, but only under certain conditions or circumstances. For example, you can have the new car but only as long as you don't get a ticket. That diamond ring ... if you lose ten pounds. The new computer, gaming console, or phone if you manage to keep up with your schoolwork.

Even love can be the same. We're loved if we smile

back. Or make our bed, prepare the meals, launder the clothes, or behave acceptably in public. It doesn't sound much like love if we must perform to receive it. If we have to be "good" before we're loved, is it really love? It's the reason adoptees into a new family will often test the love of their adoptive family by acting out in the worst way. Only when they receive proof that they won't be rejected no matter how badly they behave can they begin to trust in the love they've been told is now theirs.

We are adopted into God's family when we believe on Christ and accept his salvation. Yet, we are not immune to needing proof that God really loves us no matter what. In a human family, that proof might look like this:

Your parents make sure you have what you need, even if they have to do without. If they can put a smile on your face, they are content. In essence, they put your welfare and comfort above theirs.

Your parents give up their sleep so you can dream in safety and security. As a baby, of course, but also as you grow older. They stay up late sorting out the bills, packing for the next day's trip, or assembling your Christmas gifts.

They put their goals and hobbies on hold to allow you to pursue yours. Perhaps fewer work hours, letting yard maintenance go for an extra week, or taking you out for pizza instead of to the steak house they prefer.

They take off work or cancel a trip when you are sick. They spend hours sitting up with you, taking you to the dentist, or treating you for the scratches and bruises all children get.

You become their social life. Their old set of friends have to slot into your life, rather than you slotting into theirs. Staying up late, partying ... out the window. Life becomes about you.

They share the last slice of pie ... the last chip ... the last soda in the fridge. They don't even complain, often saying, "Take it. I'm not hungry, anyway." You believe them just as they want you to. Anyway, it's the truth, because if you want it, they no longer do.

They give up their privacy to let you crawl into bed with them when you are frightened at night. They save for your future, perhaps in a college fund, rather than for themselves. They take a deep breath when you damage something they treasure, spill an embarrassing secret, or hog the television for your latest show; and all they say is, "It's okay. It's just stuff ... information ... a TV show."

Essentially, they give you all of them without expecting you to do or be anything more than their child. That's God's unbreakable love when we come to him in repentance and ask him to cleanse us from our wrongdoing, from the times we've broken something, said the wrong thing, or taken time away from him for some silly purpose that we deemed more important.

No strings attached.

As we read in Romans 5:8, "While we were still sinners ..." God didn't hold up a hand, push us away, and say, "When you're all cleaned up ..." Rather, he reached out to us instead with, "Come just as you are. I love you already."

The ultimate freebie, and he offers it to us.

Faithful Through Our Failures

If we are faithless, He remains faithful ...

— 2 Timothy 2:13 —

Have you ever let a harsh word escape your lips, perhaps in an argument or animated discussion, and the moment you say it, you think, oops ... yet it's now out there? In the emotion of the moment, you can't process fast enough to backtrack. Instead, you barrel through to the end, spikes extended, hoping to feel vindicated at coming out on top.

You may win the argument, but you lose something in the process. Faith, trust, companionship ... and what it costs soon begins to feel like a steep price to bear. You know there's only one recourse, and that's to apologize and try to correct the damage you caused. In the best of relationships, your partner, spouse, or coworker will understand, be gracious, and let the stumble go. They will accept the situation as a glitch in a good relationship, forgive, and move forward from there.

Failure is only failure if we let it be. God says he is faithful even when we fall flat on our faces and are too embarrassed to raise our heads to face him. He wants us to reach out to him. His forgiveness is part of his unbreakable love, and he's ready to let it flow over and cover every mistake we make.

David, the biblical king, is known as a man after

God's own heart. Yet, David murdered, committed adultery, and was often filled with pride. Here's what made the difference in David's relationship with God: David repented, and God forgave him. Every. Time.

Joseph's brothers sold him into slavery, a heinous act against a sibling. God chose to use their betrayal to vault Joseph into power in the Egyptian kingdom. Joseph, acting through the forgiving nature of God, forgave them, saving them from famine as he invited them into the bounty of the king's household.

Sampson had everything. This is the man who killed a thousand Philistines with the jawbone of a donkey. Yet, he sacrificed his place in the hierarchy of Israel for the arms of a deceitful woman and lost everything, including his eyesight. Yet, he repented, and God returned his strength to him; and in the last moments of his life, Sampson killed more of the enemy than he had during all the years before.

Rahab. As a prostitute, she had a reputation in the city of Jericho. By anyone's measure, she was not a good girl. Yet, she believed in the God of the Israelites, helped the two spies sent by Joshua, and received God's protection when the time came to exact divine retribution upon the city.

Even someone especially close to Jesus, Peter, denied him three times. Jesus even knew he would do it and told him so. Yet, Jesus shared his prediction with compassion and love rather than indignation and accusation. Peter immediately repented and became a powerful leader of the early church.

Then there were those in the biblical narrative that "failed forward." They failed, but through God's unbreakable love, they received his forgiveness and went on to do wonders in his name.

Jonah is known more for his failure than his astounding successes. Yet, when Jonah repented of his disobedience, God was faithful through his failure and used Jonah to redeem an entire city.

Jacob, one of our biblical heroes … he lied and connived to get his way; and yet, God blessed him by making his sons into the twelve tribes of Israel. Why? Because God is faithful even when we stumble.

We've yet to cover Abraham who was too old to have children and Sarah who was barren. They felt like failures, but God saw them as ripe for success in his plan.

Moses had a speech impediment. It was a flaw he felt to be insurmountable. He had also killed an

Egyptian and considered himself an outcast of his people. God told him, "You, Moses, are the one I choose. Your failures are of no consequence in my plan. I will be faithful to my call on your life no matter the failures you have endured."

What do you consider to be your ultimate failure? Is it something you failed to do, something you bungled, or something that you feel is so intrinsically wrong with you that it prevents you from achieving God's best for your life? Whatever it is, God brushes his hand across your past and, like an eraser, it's all gone. God wants you to hear him say this: "I am the faithful one. You may have failed in your eyes, but I see what you can become. Join me and see what I intend to make of your life."

God is faithful through our failures.

Every time.

— 2 —

Love That Gives All

The Cross and the Heart
of the Father

*Greater love has no one than this: to lay
down one's life for one's friends.*

— John 15:13 —

Giving everything …

Like, every single thing? Try to imagine this: Yes,
you can have my music collection. Yes, every song. Or
… you want my car? Sure, here are the keys to my
truck as well.

Then there's this scenario: Of course you can empty my pantry into the trunk of your car. Please take the steaks in the freezer, too.

Who does that?

Or, to hit closer to home: Please take my children, too. That one makes us cringe, as it should. We are driven to protect our children at all times, likely with a stronger arm that we would protect ourselves.

Several years ago, a family in a small town northwest of Fort Worth, Texas, had a son diagnosed with bone cancer at a young age. His parents taught in the local schools, so they weren't rich. Over the years, the boy had a leg amputated, yet that didn't detract from his parents' determination to give him every chance possible to live his best life ever. While a senior at the local high school, the prognosis turned grim.

The boy's parents had hoped he would last long enough to at least graduate, but that didn't happen. They had invested eighteen years in their son and much of their financial resources, and he was lost, anyway. When asked if they would have done things differently if they had known he wouldn't survive, their answer was, "Absolutely not."

When we truly love, no sacrifice is too great.

That's the level of love God demonstrates for his creation.

A Father's Willing Sacrifice

For God so loved the world that He gave His one and only Son ...

— John 3:16 —

At what point is a sacrifice worth the trade? It does involve a trade, after all. In the story of the boy diagnosed with bone cancer, his parents gave their time, love, and financial resources in trade for providing their son the best opportunity possible to live a fruitful, satisfactory life. He was their son, bone and blood, part of them. Their connection was inseparable, one of the heart.

How about the trades we're willing to make for those connected to us in other ways? According to Army.mil, in 1970, in Cambodia with Company B, Sgt. Leslie Sabo was riddled with shrapnel from enemy fire, and refusing to give in, charged an enemy bunker to throw a grenade inside. He was determined to stop the enemy fire from decimating his company, and he sacrificed his life to give his comrades a chance for success.

The war history website cherrieswriter.com talks about four Army chaplains who, in 1943, knowingly sacrificed their lives to aid the 904 men on the troop transport S.S. *Dorchester* when it was hit by a U-boat near Greenland. The chaplains—two Protestants, one Catholic, and one Jewish—assisted in building life rafts and even gave away their own lifejackets as the transport disappeared beneath them.

So, back to our question … at what point is a sacrifice worth the risk? Records reveal that Chaplain First Lt. Clark V. Poling, one of the four aboard the *Dorchester*, wrote his father to request that he ask God to not simply keep him safe but to make him adequate for what would be required of him.

Adequacy. This word suggests competency … the ability to fulfill the task … and perhaps we need to include the *willingness* to fulfill the task. Not only was Poling's father willing to let his son step into the melee to perform what was required of him as a U.S. soldier, Poling desired that same willingness of himself. His request for prayer suggests that he wasn't sure he had it but that it was his greatest desire.

Before Jesus came to the earth to die on the cross, I imagine the conversation between God, the Father, and Jesus, the Son, going something like this:

"Jesus, have you been paying attention to what's going on down there?"

"Down where, Father?"

"Son, haven't you been paying attention?"

"Well, yeah, Father, but there's a lot to do in and about Heaven, and I've been very busy. What have I missed?"

"Come sit beside me and I'll show you."

Jesus joins God, and as God expects, Jesus is as distressed as God at the wreckage of morals and human connectivity that's degraded the human condition. Soon, their conversation turns to possible options to correct the situation before it goes too far.

God says, "I might need to send someone down to survey the situation. Things are looking pretty explosive about now. Those Romans, especially. They are really mucking up things with my Children."

"Yes, I can see that. The suffering must be immense. Do you think if I ... maybe?" Jesus points to himself and then down towards the earth.

"You, Jesus?" God frowns before continuing. "I don't know if you realize what you're suggesting. Did you catch the pretty explosive part? And all those crosses … the Romans are putting all manner of people on those, and it looks really gruesome. It isn't safe down there for you to go alone."

"I can do this, Father."

God thinks a moment before saying, "Perhaps if I send ten thousand angels as guards—"

"Father," and Jesus chuckles. "You know better. I must become one of them for this to work. That's not likely if I constantly have security guards all around me. And regardless of the risk, I can do this. You've made me adequate for this, and I'm willing."

"Even if you wind up on one of those crosses?" God shakes his head in disbelief.

"Especially if I wind up on one of those crosses."

There's no record of this conversation in the Bible, but it's clear in the Word that Jesus and God agreed on Jesus taking human form and spending 33 years bonding with the human race and dying on one of the Roman crosses. And here's the vital part of this: God was willing to let Jesus go, and Jesus was willing to take up the challenge … even when he knew it would culminate in his death on the cross.

What prompted God to begin this chain of events? "For God so loved the world that He gave His one and only Son, that whosoever believes in Him should not perish but have eternal life."

That's the heart of our God. He was willing to sacrifice his most prized possession—his Son—for us to have salvation. He still loves us that much today.

The Son Who Took Our Place

He loved us and sent His Son as an atoning sacrifice ...

— I John 4:10 —

In the novel *A Tale of Two Cities* by Charles Dickens, one of the great classics of all time, the Englishman Sydney Carton switches places with French aristocrat Charles Darnay, who is about to be executed during the French Revolution.

Carton, who as an Englishman, is free to live the rest of his life outside of the travesties of the French Revolution, tosses away his options to let another man, Darnay, escape the executioner. Darnay, then, receives the postponement of his sentence and the freedom to continue to live his life as he sees fit.

In the novel, what motivates Carton to do this? Social justice? Outrage at the ruthlessness of the French Revolution? Neither of those. Carton makes his sacrifice for love. In the novel, Carton has one great love, Lucie Manette, who has married Darnay. He knows he can never have her, but he can sacrifice himself for her happiness.

Under the biblical Old Covenant, yearly sacrifices were a part of life, standard fare, with the rules written down so that no one could claim, "Oh, I have to do what? No one ever told me."

Then there were the priests from the tribe of Levi. These Levitical priests claimed their jobs by birthright, not by inclination or skill. As the older generations gave way and new priests rose to fulfill the role of intermediary between man and God, sometimes they veered offline, even leading the people astray with loose teachings.

These earthly priests were men filled with human desires and weaknesses, so much so that their first requirement upon entering the Temple was to offer sacrifices for their own sins before they could make the animal sacrifices for the sins of the people. They could only enter the Holy of Holies once a year, and they had to perform these rites over and over, year after year.

These Levitical sacrifices served as waystations, stops along the way, and they were pointers to the Messiah, who was Jesus, and who would be the perfect sacrifice for all mankind.

Here's what makes Jesus different from the Levitical priests:

Jesus was chosen by God to be the ultimate priest due to his personal qualifications (Heb. 7:11-22).

Jesus became a permanent priest. He never dies and never has to groom a replacement for his position (Heb. 7:23-25).

Jesus has no sin and can take our sins directly before God. He does not need to offer a sacrifice for himself (Heb. 7:26-27).

Jesus ministers to us and for us in a heavenly setting (Heb. 8:1-5).

Jesus ministers to us under the New Covenant rather than the Old Covenant (Heb. 8:6-13).

The priests could only enter the Most Holy Place

once a year. Jesus enters freely, at any time, to minister there on our behalf (Heb. 9:11-24).

Jesus made the final sacrifice, one that never has to be repeated (Heb. 9:25-10:24).

Sydney Carton thought his sacrifice beneficial to one other person, and because of his love for her, gave up his life.

The Levitical priests viewed their position in the Temple as a job, one they performed at varying levels of proficiency ... over and over, year after year.

Jesus became the ultimate priest. His sacrifice outshone all other sacrifices. In his perfection, through the New Testament Covenant, he takes our sins directly before God and lays them before the Father. Jesus' sacrifice is so much better than the temporary sacrifices offered by the Levitical priests. His death on the cross did what those sacrifices could never do. They made the forgiveness of sin possible in a final, once-and-for-all manner, so that the same level of sacrifice would never be necessary again.

The Old Covenant was only ever meant to be a waystation in God's plan for humanity. With the coming of Jesus, it is no longer necessary and no longer in effect. We can now draw near to God

through his Son with the full assurance of the forgiveness of our sins when we accept Jesus as our
savior.

Love Poured Out on a Cross

*God's love has been poured out into our
hearts ...*

— Romans 5:5 —

When Jesus took our place on the cross, all future
history was changed. Instead of humanity having to
suffer under the burden of its sin, we instead got to
revel in God's unbroken love poured out through his
Son's death on the cross.

The first level of love that flowed from and
through the death of Jesus was sacrificial love. Death
is the ultimate act of self-sacrifice. There is no coming
back, no undoing of the deed, no way to: *Oops, let's
try that again.* Jesus willingly gave his life for
humanity that he might atone for our sins and recon-
cile us with the Father. His sacrificial death demonstrated the true depth of God's unbroken love for his

creation.

The next level of love is that of forgiving love. God is a good and loving god. He is the supreme force in the heavens and on the earth. He wants to do good things for his children, including offering us forgiveness when we turn unto him. The cross is his testament to his forgiving nature. Jesus' sacrifice is his way of creating a path to forgive our sins and restore our relationship with him.

Jesus' time on the cross also demonstrates God's redeeming love. Jesus, through his sacrifice and death, provided redemption from sin and death. When we choose his salvation, we receive eternal life and a new beginning.

Jesus also revealed God's loving compassion for the travesty that humanity had become. Part of God's plan was to understand the depths of humanity's despair, to connect to each type of temptation man endured, and to truly set an example for all men to follow. The suffering and pain of humanity is wrapped up in the travails Jesus endured, proving that he knows the pain of what it is to be human

Jesus, through the cross and his resurrection, loved with a powerful love that overcomes. Every sin, every temptation, every agonizing experience leading up to the crucifixion ... Our Lord overcame the most brutal injustice and cruelty.

Through his sacrifice, Jesus set the example for agape love. In his death, he embodied a love that is unconditional, selfless, and sacrificial. He never told the disciples, "If you do this ..." or "If you do that ..." He loved Judas when he brought the Roman soldiers to the Garden; he loved Peter when he denied him three times; he loved the Roman soldier who pierced him in the side. Jesus loved so unconditionally with agape love that even at the Last Supper, none of the other disciples suspected Judas, even though Jesus knew all along.

God's love that flowed through Jesus on the cross also formed a foundational love. From the day of Jesus' crucifixion, the Christian church established a foothold on the earth. From that leaping off point, Jesus' followers were inspired to follow their Master's example and love one another as Jesus had loved them.

Jesus' death was, additionally, love in action. From his respectful words as he stood before Pilate to his accepting endurance as he endured the thirty-nine lashes, Jesus acted out his love. He carried his cross, let the Roman soldiers lash him to the tree, and invited the thief at his side to join him in heaven. He called out to God and forgave his tormentors, even as he gave up his life on the cross.

The love of God that flowed through Jesus is a love that has endured. Even as he heard the sounds and felt the pain of his approaching death, Jesus' love never wavered. Even in the Garden, when Peter cut off the ear of the servant of the high priest, Jesus felt compassion and love and healed the man's injury.

Finally, the love of God through Jesus transcends all limitations. It's been two thousand years since Christ walked the earth, and still, the example of love that he demonstrated during his life and death resounds as loudly today as it did then. His love is unlimited by space, for there is no place on the earth mankind can travel that the love of God cannot reach. His love offers us eternal life and a relationship with him, if only we choose to accept his salvation.

Thank God that his Son's sacrifice became a vessel of his love poured out upon all humanity. With his sacrifice, I am forgiven, you are forgiven, and everyone who comes to him is forgiven. However, without the cross, humanity would still be lost.

The Nails Were Not Enough

No one takes it from me, but I lay it down of my own accord.

— John 10:18 —

If you remember our fictional conversation between God and Jesus about sending someone to investigate the rowdiness occurring on the earth, you'll recall God's suggestion that Jesus take with him ten thousand angels as bodyguards. Instead, Jesus came alone and spent a lifetime revealing his dedication to loving humanity, to not prioritizing himself but always putting those in need first.

He demonstrated one of his most profound declarations of love for humanity as he hung on the cross. As his body bled and he gasped for air—the cross was about suffocation, an extremely painful death—he called out in Luke 23:34, "Father, forgive them, for they do not know what they are doing."

We also have the story of Lazarus. The timing of Lazarus' death gives us an archetypal example of the death and resurrection that will soon take place in Jesus' own life, yet the true emotion that flowed from Jesus when he heard of his friend's condition reveals his true love and compassion for humanity.

Jesus also took time from his ministry to look out for the hurting and needy among his contemporaries. We can read multiple stories of Jesus healing the sick, touching the eyes of the blind, washing the leper clean, and reaching out to the Centurion's servant. Jesus' time wasn't about him, but what people needed from him.

Jesus didn't overlook injustice and prejudice. Take the example of the woman at the well, or the woman who was being stoned. He invited Zacchaeus to come out of the tree—a tax collector, someone despised by the Jews—and dine with him. He also decried the selling of sacrificial animals in the Temple and even overturned the tables of those buying and selling.

Jesus was especially attuned to those whose lives were impacted by evil spirits. The New Testament mentions as many as fifty-five times Jesus casts out evil spirits, although only five are described in detail. He casts out seven demons from Mary Magdalene, one from a man in the synagogue, and several from men near the tombs, where the demons even acknowledged Jesus as the Son of God.

Jesus had an affinity for people who were marginalized by the society of his day. The blind, the lepers, the lame, they were important to him. He also reached out to those outside Jewish cultural and religious boundaries, such as the Samaritans and Canaanites. He healed Peter's mother-in-law and a woman suffering from a hemorrhage, and he invited the children, a group often pushed aside or ignored, to gather around him, for he knew the importance of reaching out to those who would one day guide the affairs of the world.

Jesus described his body and his blood as the covenant of salvation at the Last Supper. Then, on the cross, he followed through. He allowed nothing to divert God's plan to bring salvation to humanity.

As an example of his humility and willingness to live out the plan of God for his life, Jesus knelt to wash the feet of each of his disciples. He did the simple thing that seemed abhorrent to his followers but one that he knew would make a soul-searing impact upon them when they remembered his life with them. His example would compel them to treat each other with compassion and grace, for Jesus had lived it out before them.

We can't overlook Jesus' willingness to be crucified. He prayed through the night while his disciples slept, choosing to accept the fate his Father had assigned him, death on the cross, one of the most painful ways to die known to the Roman overlords. While he could have said no, he chose to say yes. This revealed his determination to act as a bridge to the redemption of humanity.

Jesus' most soul-searing example of making a choice to remain on the cross and his ultimate act of love and sacrifice is his acceptance of the punishment for all the sins of humanity. As God turns his face away at the moment of his death, Jesus lets the pain roll over him, taking it in to become our path for reconciliation with God.

The nails were never enough to hold Jesus on the cross. His arms and feet were not bound by the hands of the Roman soldiers. He could have called on the heavenly host to release him and lift him to the foot of his Father's throne.

His love for mankind was the thing that held him there.

Love Stronger Than Death

*For love is as strong as death ... like blazing
fire, like the very flame of the Lord.*

— Song of Solomon 8:6 —

Yes, Jesus was buried. At least, his body was. We
read in Matthew 27:57-60 about Jospeh from
Arimathea who asked Pilate for the body of Jesus.
Jesus was wrapped in linen in a tomb and a great stone
was rolled across the entrance.

Yet, Jesus wasn't in that tomb. He had a job to do.
He visited the spirit world and preached to those who
had suffered from disbelief in the days of Noah
(I Peter 3:18-20). He visited Paradise and, while
there, he took the righteous dead with him to be in
heaven (Luke 23:43).

Jesus' descent into the spirit world (and his
eventual resurrection from the dead) symbolizes his
victory over death and sin. His example of preaching
to the spirits from the distant past illustrates the
application of the gospel message to provide salvation

to all who believe.

Just to be certain that Jesus' body didn't "disappear" by unscrupulous means, once Joseph of Arimathea placed the body in the tomb, Matthew 27:62-66 tells of Pilate assigning a guard of Roman soldiers to ensure that the dead remained "dead." Little did they understand that they weren't simply guarding a dead body. This was Jesus we're talking about!

The urgency by Joseph to ensure that Jesus was buried promptly was motivated by the timing of the Jewish Sabbath. At sundown on the day of Jesus' crucifixion, the Sabbath started, and the next day was a day of rest and worship. Only after the Sabbath was completed could anyone visit the tomb and tend to the body of Jesus (Mark 15:42-47). On the morning of the third day, which the modern church celebrates as Easter Sunday, the Bible commonly mentions four women visiting the tomb to anoint the body of Jesus:

Mary Magdalene, who is listed in all four gospels. She is sometimes described as a follower of Jesus who was present at his crucifixion and burial.

Mary, the mother of James, who is also listed in all four gospels. She is sometimes referred to as the mother of James the Less or the mother of Joses.

Salome is mentioned by name in the book of Mark and in other places as the mother of James and John, who are two of Jesus' disciples.

Johanna, described as a follower of Jesus who was present at his crucifixion and burial, is mentioned by name in the book of Luke.

Other women are also mentioned, including Mary, the mother of Jesus. These women, all of them, play an important role in the events of the resurrection, for it is by their witness that the stone is rolled away and the tomb is empty!

Jesus not only appears to these women as a testimony of his resurrection but also to two of his disciples in Luke 24:13-35.

> *Now that same day two of them were going to a village called Emmaus, about seven miles from Jerusalem. ¹⁴ They were talking with each other about everything that had happened. ¹⁵ As they talked and discussed these things with each other, Jesus himself came up and walked along with them; ¹⁶ but they were kept from recognizing him.*

^17 He asked them, "What are you discussing together as you walk along?"

They stood still, their faces downcast. ^18 One of them, named Cleopas, asked him, "Are you the only one visiting Jerusalem who does not know the things that have happened there in these days?"

^19 "What things?" he asked.

"About Jesus of Nazareth," they replied. "He was a prophet, powerful in word and deed before God and all the people. ^20 The chief priests and our rulers handed him over to be sentenced to death, and they crucified him; ^21 but we had hoped that he was the one who was going to redeem Israel. And what is more, it is the third day since all this took place. ^22 In addition, some of our women amazed us. They went to the tomb early this morning ^23 but didn't find his body. They came and told us that they had seen a vision of angels, who said he was alive. ^24 Then some of our companions went to the tomb and found it just as the women had said, but they did not see Jesus."

^25 He said to them, "How foolish you are,

and how slow to believe all that the prophets have spoken! ²⁶ Did not the Messiah have to suffer these things and then enter his glory?" ²⁷ And beginning with Moses and all the Prophets, he explained to them what was said in all the Scriptures concerning himself.

²⁸ As they approached the village to which they were going, Jesus continued on as if he were going farther. ²⁹ But they urged him strongly, "Stay with us, for it is nearly evening; the day is almost over." So he went in to stay with them.

³⁰ When he was at the table with them, he took bread, gave thanks, broke it and began to give it to them. ³¹ Then their eyes were opened and they recognized him, and he disappeared from their sight. ³² They asked each other, "Were not our hearts burning within us while he talked with us on the road and opened the Scriptures to us?"

³³ They got up and returned at once to Jerusalem. There they found the Eleven and those with them, assembled together ³⁴ and saying, "It is true! The Lord has risen and has

appeared to Simon." [35] *Then the two told what had happened on the way, and how Jesus was recognized by them when he broke the bread.*

Jesus, during his life and his death, was filled with the unbreakable love of his Father toward humanity. His strength flowed from his bond with his Father and his divine nature as the eternal Son of the almighty God and the Risen Savior of all mankind. His was a love stronger than death and would jump-start the Great Commission to spread the good news of the gospel throughout the world (Matt. 28:18-20).

— 3 —

Loved Into Wholeness

Healing the Wounded Heart

He heals the brokenhearted and binds up their wounds.

— Psalm 147:3 —

Even when we can't see the pain, wounded hearts surround us. This invisible breakdown of mental health can come from divorce; childhood trauma; an unexpected health diagnosis; the loss of financial security; or the loss of a loved one.

The security of our lives evaporates around us, frittered away into trauma and tears. It seems no one understands … and the hours stretch into days. We feel as if they will never end.

We see this played out in 2 Kings 4:18-37 with the Shunammite woman. At first, things are great. After many years of wishing for a child, she and her husband are blessed with a son. You can imagine the joys she treasures up during his childhood: his first words, his first steps, all the things any parent stores away in their heart times ten because she desired him for so long.

Then, it falls apart. Her son falls ill, perhaps with a cough at first, then an upset stomach. The Bible tells us in verse 18 that the boy says to his father, "Oh, my head, my head!" Whatever the illness, the woman is helpless as she watches him grow weaker and weaker. The security of her role as a mother crumbles around her, leaving a void that seems as dark as the night sky as he dies in her arms.

She seeks help from the prophet Elisha, confident in her grief that the man of God is the answer to the evil that has befallen her. Our key verse for this chapter says: "He [the Christ] heals the brokenhearted and binds up their wounds." In the story in 2 Kings, Elisha breathes life back into the dead child, and he is well once again. The Shunammite woman's faith in the restorative power of God becomes tangible in her arms as she holds her young son once more.

Whatever the hurt you bear, this is what God wants to do for you—heal your wounded heart.

Love That Knows Your Name

I have called you by name; you are mine.

— Isaiah 43:1 —

It's easy in today's Christian world to equate salvation with a blessed life. No troubles, no worries, God is my Redeemer, and there is always sunshine on the horizon.

There's no way that's biblical. The Bible is strewn with people who were broken, troubled, or even downright devious. Even so, God's love reached out to them, called them by name, and lifted them to greater heights than they had known before.

We think of Abraham as the great patriarch. His

faith in God was the beginning of a great nation. After all, he is known for his obedience to God's command to sacrifice his son, Isaac, only to be given a reprieve when a ram is caught in a nearby bramble. Yet, Abraham also suffered instances of dishonesty and doubt. God loved and blessed him anyway.

Jacob ... oh, my, what a tale we can tell here. The man was a deceiver who tricked his brother, Esau, and his father, Abraham, out of the birthright that rightfully should have gone to Esau. Yet, today we know Jacob for his eventual transformation into a man of incredible faith in God who becomes the patriarch of the twelve tribes of Israel.

Joseph, a man of integrity beyond question, yet he was sold as a slave and endured years in prison for a crime he didn't commit. God honored his faithfulness with a powerful position of leadership in Egypt.

Moses, overcome with doubt and hindered by a speech impediment ... the man was doomed to be a failure. Yet, God knew Moses by name and called him from the burning bush to lead the Israelites to deliverance from their Egyptian oppressors.

David, the principal author of the Psalms, a man after God's own heart ... and known for adultery, murder, and other sins. God saw David's heart, called him by his name, and lifted him out of each of his troubles.

Elijah was despondent and suicidal. God reached out to him, and today our faith is built up by the life of the prophet.

Jonah and the whale (or the big fish), and a city needing the redemption of God. Through God's love, Jonah realized his disobedience and ministered to the city of Ninevah. The population of that city turned to God and avoided impending destruction.

Rahab, a prostitute, was spared when the walls of Jericho were destroyed by the hand of God.

Mary Magdalene, a woman of questionable morals, now a follower of Jesus. She attended his crucifixion and resurrection and is today a reminder of the redemptive love of God.

And Paul. This is the most poignant and telling example of God speaking to us by name. In the book of Acts, God blinds Paul (at the time known as Saul) while on the road to Damascus and asks, "Saul, Saul, why are you persecuting me?" God then gives Saul a revelation of the divine nature of Jesus and commissions him to preach the gospel to the gentiles as well as the Jews. As a new believer and a freshly minted apostle, Saul takes the name of Paul to reflect his Roman citizenship and burgeoning missionary style of ministry.

Each of the people on this list suffered, some without justification or cause, while others seemed to be their own worst enemy. Yet, God saw through each person's pain, called them by name, and loved them into wholeness. God took their broken situation, wrapped them in his love, and said, "I've got this. I'm here for you. I will mend your wounded heart and lift you to greater heights than you have known. Trust in me, my child."

Where do you fall among these biblical giants? Which of them do you most identify with? Which ones seem to have borne the pain you carry inside? Joseph, unjustly accused? Or Mary Magdalene, with a past you carry with you? Perhaps Jacob, a person with great possibilities but unable to speak the truth to save his life. Jonah, filled with the arrogance of disobedience … Moses, feeling like a failure … David, stumbling over and over … Elijah, tired of life and wanting a way out … who are you inside, the person no one except God sees?

God knows your name. His love is available to heal your wounds. Will you answer him today?

Love That Sees the Hurt

I have seen the misery of my people. ... I am concerned about their suffering.

— Exodus 3:7 —

Nicky Cruz is a name that inspires many Christians. If you've never heard of him, let me tell you some of his story.

Cruz had a rough beginning in a tough neighborhood in Puerto Rico. His parents practiced witchcraft, and his own mother called him the "Son of Satan" during a spiritual trance. He attempted suicide at age nine and was banished to live with his brother in New York at the age of fifteen.

Then things went downhill for Nicky Cruz.

He joined a gang called the Mau Maus, and his best friend (and fellow gang member) died in his arms. He seemed destined for prison and worse ... except.

Into Cruz's life steps David Wilkerson, a skinny preacher filled with relentless love. Wilkerson later writes *The Cross and the Switchblade*, a book about his experiences with the gangs of New York City, including Nicky Cruz, the then-leader of the Mau Maus. You can also find the story of Nicky Cruz in the film *Run Baby Run* about his life and conversion to Christianity.

Here's what I want you to take from the story of Nicky Cruz. God saw the misery of Cruz's hurtful and hurting life. He sent David Wilkerson, and through Wilkerson, God loved Cruz into wholeness. He healed Cruz's wounds and brought him to redemption in Jesus. Now, Cruz ministers to others who are hurting so that God can continue to love the hurting into wholeness.

The book of Exodus centers around the freeing of the Israelites from Egypt. As the third chapter begins, Moses, filled with self-doubt, is tending sheep in the wilderness near Horeb, known as the mountain of God. God calls out of a burning bush, "Moses, Moses!"

God knew just where to find Moses. Moses had run from the Egyptian palace, from the murder of an

Egyptian, and from the mocking voices of his people. He thought he was leading a life hidden in Midian and invisible to the world. He wanted to disappear, and he thought he had. Yet, God stepped in and called him by name.

To understand the importance of this, Moses was not a happy man. He had grown up in the palaces of Egypt with all the benefits that offered. He was given the honor of being raised as a son of the Pharoah's daughter. Yet, he is now in the wilderness, despondent and filled with shame. He is so self-defeating that when he hears God's voice, he hides his face and replies, "Who am I? Send someone else."

Moses had no confidence at all. He was suffering, and God knew that. And in his love for his people, God called him anyway. However, there's a second part to this story. God had seen the suffering of the Israelites at the hands of the Egyptians, and he had a plan to heal their wounded hearts, also. Verse 7 says, "I have surely seen the affliction of my people who are in Egypt and have heard their cry because of their taskmasters. I know their sufferings."

Do you feel invisible? Do you wear a mask so that no one can tell how much you hurt? Does your pain crush you inside and drain all the emotions and empathy from you? God sees your hurt. He knows your misery. He wants to take your suffering and sooth it with his love. God says to you, "I have seen what you've endured. I know where you are, and I want to wrap you in my love. I want to heal your wounded heart."

Give it up to him. Let him have control. When You feel those negative emotions rolling over you once again, reach out to God and let him be the light in your darkness, the redemption in your sorrow, and the balm to your brokenness.

The God Who Draws Near

The Lord is close to the brokenhearted . . .

— Psalm 34:18 —

Emotional pain is a crippling cudgel that batters us repeatedly. Soon, we feel we can no longer face the life we must endure. This verse in Psalms finishes with, ". . . and saves those who are crushed in spirit."

The first thing to take from this verse is that God

knows how you feel. He senses your pain. He sent his Son to the earth to experience what you and I feel. He acted as a human sponge that soaked up the detritus of what humanity had become and took that experience with him when he returned to the Father. Jesus, who is one with the Father, can understand your pain because he experienced it during his time on the earth. This poignant and life-affirming verse emphasizes the hope and comfort that God wants to provide to heal your wounded heart.

So, make a list of your life's challenges. Add in losses you feel you've suffered. Don't leave anything out. All of them are important to God. Then add in the personal struggles you wrestle with, everything that causes you deep emotional distress and suffering. Some things on this list might stir up past pain as they unseal old memories you thought boxed up and safely stored at the back of a mental shelf, memories that once left you brokenhearted and crushed in spirit.

As you read over your list, it's important to remember the first four words in this verse. "The Lord is close …" This phrase highlights the unwavering presence of God wherever you are in your walk, whether during family trauma or when a health diagnosis upsets every plan you've made. Remember the family whose son was diagnosed with bone cancer? After they received that devastating news, everything changed for them. All their priorities turned topsy-turvy. What they'd placed high on their list of goals flew out the window, and they had to reevaluate where life was taking them.

As Christians, we must place our trust in God's unwavering presence and attention. Our Lord sees us where we are. He focuses on our needs, even when we are so walled in by despair that we can only see darkness. Even when the black skies of impending doom swallow the joy of walking with Christ, God is actively engaged in bringing us to redemption. He is constantly and consistently with us even in our darkest moments.

God wants to save those who are crushed in spirit. The very reason he sent Jesus as the redemption for our sins was his love for his creation. We read in the Bible how God treasures the birds and the flowers of the field, and he does. They are essential elements of his divine efforts to build a world environment that will engage us and give us joy. If God places so much concern and care in the flora and fauna of the world in an effort to provide an attractive and well-balanced home for his children, how can we not know that he has even greater love and concern for those who inhabit that world?

This verse is God offering us comfort and hope through the Christ who offered his life on the cross to bring a direct connection between God and man. In this connection, we find the salvation that returns us to unity with God. If you are experiencing emotional pain, this is your opportunity. God offers you comfort. You can access his comfort through time in the Word and in meaningful prayer.

God also wants your healing. He offers healing for physical needs and for emotional pain. Both are very real. We can often see the physical needs, hold them up for others to evaluate, show them as proof that we need God's touch. Emotional pain is harder to offer to God. We're told to "try harder," to "buck up," or to "be a man" (or a woman). We choose to put on a brave face and let ourselves fall apart in our private space.

God says he will come to our aid. He assures us of his comfort and encourages us to seek solace in his presence and his ability to save us from whatever calamity besets us, for "he is close to the broken-hearted ..."

You Are Not Disqualified

Who shall separate us from the love of Christ?

— Romans 8:35 —

Have you ever run a marathon? It's a long-distance foot race often set on public roadways and requires participants to cover an exact distance.

26 miles plus 2/10s to be specific.

The marathon can be on trail routes, and accommodations can be made for those in wheelchairs. You can walk or run, but most marathons have a course time limit, meaning you must complete the distance before the clock expires or you don't get a prize. Organizers usually allow 6-8 hours for the race.

Here's what I want you to pull from this: A marathon operates by a set of established rules. Don't follow the rules, and you don't have a marathon.

That doesn't mean the work you put in is any less.

It still takes months of training, agonizing hours on the course, and days (or weeks) of recovery. No one wants to put in the effort without the possibility of winning—or at least completing—the race.

In Atlanta in 2025, over 11,000 runners participated in the Publix Atlanta Marathon. There were 11,000 people who had spent months training, many of whom had to travel to Atlanta, pay for accommodations, and sacrifice a portion of their life, only to complete the race and realize they were disqualified.

Every single runner. Disqualified. No credit given for all the hard work they'd invested in completing the race. It was the largest turnout since 2020, and it was a colossal disappointment.

What happened? Atlanta is one of the fastest growing megalopolises in the nation, making road construction endemic to life in Atlanta. Due to road construction, several cones along the course were misplaced in Grant Park at about the 20-mile mark, and the course came up short. 554 feet short, disqualifying everyone who participated.

All 11,000. Ouch.

Hebrews 12:1-4 compares our Christian life to a

race, essentially telling us we are running a marathon. It gives us some rules that we must follow to successfully reach the end.

1. We must discard worldly weights and sin.
2. We must run with endurance.
3. We must look unto Jesus.

Leave out any of these rules, and on judgement day, when we stand before God, he will ask, "Did you cover every mile ... even the final 554 feet? Let me check the record ..."

Here's where Rule 3 comes in. When we come to Jesus and choose him to be the author and finisher of our faith, he opens the book of our life, and he looks over what we've done, where we've traveled, and what we have yet to complete, and he says, "Hmm. This looks like this section needs adjusting. I can't erase any of what's happened, but I can put my own stamp on the record."

Then, he inks up his Jesus stamp, and stamp, stamp, the name of Jesus obliterates any infractions in our race. Mistakes we made, stamp, stamp, only the name of Jesus remains. Things we didn't quite get done ... stamp, stamp, that hole is filled in with the name of Our Lord. People we hurt, offerings we failed to give, the times we let other people down, stamp, stamp, and God says, "Here's what I found when I checked the record: the name of Jesus stamped everywhere! Your record is complete! You get full and unadulterated credit for finishing the race! Welcome to the finish line. Enter in, you good and faithful servant."

We are never disqualified when we run the race with Jesus at our side. Our verse asks the question: "Who shall separate us from the love of Christ?" There's only one answer, and we must take it to heart.

NO ONE.

There is no one who can separate us from the love of Christ. Jesus proved his love on the cross, and through his sacrifice, he provides the channel for God to love us into wholeness and heal our wounded heart.

Beauty from Ashes

[God will] provide for those who grieve in Zion—to bestow on them a crown of beauty instead of ashes.

— Isaiah 61:3 —

This iconic verse from the book of Isaiah returns to us vibrantly at the beginning of Jesus' ministry as he proclaims himself to be the fulfillment of this prophecy. Isaiah's words describe the archetypal Messianic deliverer, an ideal that Israel held up against all others, a perfection that caused anyone else to pale in comparison.

Chapter 61:1 says, "He has sent me ... to proclaim liberty to the captives and the opening of the prison to those who are bound." Isaiah's words must have sounded like unbridled redemption bridging the ups and downs of the cyclic rollercoaster of Israelite history. With these words, Isaiah paints the Messiah as the transformer of sorrow and the bringer of joy.

Imagine Job, who lived a life of purity but had everything stripped from him. Job 2:8 tells us that Job sat among the ashes and scraped his skin with a pottery shard. The ashes symbolize mortality, grief, and humility. They stand for repentance from sin and wrongdoing, whether by intent or omission. They were also sprinkled on those who were "unclean" to make them ceremonially "clean."

Spiritually, ashes represent the earth, the dustiness

of what was and what no longer is, the life, hopes, and joy of what we are leaving behind. They are the sins we are no longer forced to carry. They contain our regret, repentance, and the need for reconciliation.

Essentially, they remind us that we are mortal. Our efforts on the earth are limited, and one day we will return to the beauty and unbounding love that is our creator: God.

The ashes of life express our sorrow and mourning for what we have lost. When we hold the ashes of our life, in them we see the house that a natural disaster took from us, we mourn the marriage that crumbled into divorce, and we remember the health we enjoyed before a doctor's prognosis started us down the long road of decline.

Yet, this verse tells us we will receive beauty from our ashes. How is that? When our life has crumbled around us, how can it ever be restored?

Imagine a forest interspersed with meadows. It's beautiful, and we want to maintain its beauty for everyone to enjoy. Then, one day in a thunderstorm, a lightning strike ignites a fire. The flames run rampant through the forest, consuming the underbrush and blackening the meadows.

Is all lost? No, of course not. The ashes from the flames do something for the soil, and soon new life peeks through. The newly exposed ground welcomes the sun and allows new growth to thrive.

That's the beauty God offers us. We often get weighed down by the foliage of life. The things we allow to grow up around us are so pervasive that we don't even realize how much they are stifling us. The canopy of the trees that form our life blocks the sun from the forest floor ... the brambles overtaking the meadows choke out new grasses ... it looks good from a distance, but life inside who we are is choking us spiritually, and we can't see how to get back into the sun.

Beauty instead of ashes. Beauty to ashes. Beauty from ashes. Sprinkle ashes on your lawn, and your grass will be nourished and thrive. There are still nutrients in the ashes, although they are no longer alive. Too much, and you'll kill the grass, but a light coating is a game changer for exponential growth. It's the reason the slopes of a volcano are fertile for growing pretty much anything, yet during an eruption, too much ash can bury villages and suffocate entire biomes.

God says he will give you a crown of beauty instead of ashes. What has weighed you down, he will wash away. A little of those ashes—the occasional memory that reminds you of how far you've come—will help you grow taller and stronger in God, and through his love, you will become whole.

God will have healed your wounded heart, and you will be complete in him.

— 4 —

Love Without Limits

The Boundless Reach of God's Affection

How wide and long and high and deep is the love of Christ.

— Ephesians 3:18 —

The 2019 book, *My Wilderness Experience,* by South Texas pastor Apolonio Garcia, tells his life story of feeling outside the reach of anything resembling God's love during his formative years. He had a father he worshipped . . . when he could ignore the stench of alcohol and tobacco. During long nights at home, violence often erupted between his father and his mother. Through the years, Garcia's father taught his young son how to walk the long, dark road leading to eventual murder and prison. *Devastation* is the word Garcia uses to describe the future about to slam him in the face.

Then, in stepped God through the presence of a preacher with a prison ministry who wouldn't take no from an incarcerated murderer for an answer. Where man had written off Apolonio Garcia, tossing him off as garbage to be burned, God saw an opportunity to exhibit his divine love. Through the determination of that godly pastor and the divine love of a caring God, today Garcia pastors a church while raising a family with his wife. He is the first to say that God's love is without limits, and no one is beyond the reach of God's affection.

Across Every Border

After this I looked, and there before me was a
great multitude that no one could count,
from every nation, tribe, people and language,

standing before the throne and before the Lamb.

— Revelation 7:9 —

Jesus was born into a world of borders, and not just political ones. The world of the first century was fraught with dangers that we can hardly imagine. A location ten miles away might as well be a hundred. It was easily a day's travel or more. People often lived their lives in the villages in which they were born, as any sort of meaningful travel opened the possibilities of theft, abduction, and murder.

Often, the very fact that a mountain bordered the fields around your house meant that what was past them was forever unknown. Just as today, countries could and did put up barriers to prevent people from crossing their borders. The Great Wall of China is one. In other places, bridges over rivers were guarded, with checkpoints in mountain passes. These and more divided territories and restricted movement and ideas.

Natural, geographical barriers such as rivers or oceans were even more instrumental in preventing a connection with anyone outside your small cadre of familiar people and things.

Of course, the social barriers of the day were often impossible to cross. The Samaritan woman was crippled with shame when she compared herself to her Jewish superiors. The Pharisees ... the Sadducees ... the priests in the Temple ... and the beggars on the streets. As Rudyard Kipling once wrote, "Never the twain shall meet." The people of Jesus' day were as cut off from one another as if they lived on opposite sides of the Great Wall.

The barriers of wealth inequity and lack of access to resources also drew sharp lines between the people of the day. These were magnified by socioeconomic disparities throughout the region. The leaders, priests, and those with wealth saw no benefit in mingling with the commoners groveling in poverty.

Differing languages also drove men apart. If you've ever spent time with someone from a culture that doesn't speak your language, you know how frustrating that can be. Something so simple as remarking on the weather can be a walk in the dark through a room filled with broken glass. Imagine trying to share God's message of love and salvation across that unfamiliar cultural chasm. Misunderstandings abound, and the language potholes are so great you could disappear inside.

Then bring political conflicts into the mix, and everything becomes shouting and threats. Picture the story of the Jews at Masada or the more recent events in Israel with the 140-square-mile enclave of Gaza. If food, services, and basic medical services can't cross the border, how can we hope to spread the love of God to those on the other side?

Yet, our verse from Revelation says that before the throne of the Lamb we will find "a great multitude that no one could count, from every nation, tribe, people and language." White, Black, Palestinian, Jewish, male, female, rich, poor … all and everything in between. How can this be? It all comes back to the Great Commission, what we sometimes refer to as the Call of Christ.

"Therefore go and make disciples of all nations, baptizing them in the name of the Father and of the Son and of the Holy Spirit, and teaching them to obey everything I have commanded you" (Matt. 28:19-20).

All nations. God doesn't say to stop spreading his love at the mountain range to the west. We can't choose to preach only to the rich or to the poor.

Ethnic differences ... tossed aside. Political barriers are things to be cracked wide. Geographical barriers ... build a boat, charter an airplane, send the message over the airways ... just get it done!

When we enter heaven, we will walk through the pearly gates hand in hand and arm in arm. God will look upon our heart, not our clothing, bank balance, or political affiliation. He will weigh the love we showed to one another, and in the balance of his hands, he will call us worthy or send us away.

Borders are made for God's love to break down, flow through, and minister to those on the other side. His love wants to flow across each one.

Beyond Human Understanding

The peace [love] of God, which transcends all understanding, will guard your hearts and your minds in Christ Jesus.

— Philippians 4:7 —

What sparks a human brain into life? What's the magic for consciousness, for self-awareness, and for knowing how to imagine things greater than our surroundings? Scientists, of course, can give us the neurological processes, write them out with marker-and-board, and explain them with precision and in detail. Yet, the why or the essence ... that's a different matter. We might as well throw up our hands and shrug, as no one can say definitively. It's as easy to make our couch sit up and carry on a meaningful conversation with us.

Yet God says, "I understand. I started it, and I know how to make it work to your advantage. Trust me. I love you very much and will do nothing to harm you."

But, we think, the universe. It's so wide and getting wider with each new telescope we build. The scale and complexity of it all ... where do we start? True, we have in our grasp the concepts of physics as we understand them, but matter's origins, the beginning of the cosmos, *even the possibility of other dimensions*—what? *Additional dimensions within the cosmos that we cannot delve into, manipulate, or explain in exacting detail?* Current scientific theory leans that way. Humanity experiences three such dimensions, those of length, width, and height. There's a fourth, time, but even the experts agree it's beyond our normal sense of perception and understanding.

Perhaps any theorized dimensions out there are simply additional facets of a transcendent and limitless God.

The Word says that for now we see as through a glass darkly (I Cor. 13:12). The truth is unknowable, and our understanding will only come in the fullness of time. Perhaps one day, God will sit with us and explain the M Theory that unifies all consistent versions of superstring theory, telling us that when he created all matter with his spoken word, the superstrings at the core of everything vibrated matter into being ... hence, bringing the worlds into existence at his command. He will share how his divine, unbroken love flows without limits through the mysterious substance known as dark matter and is even more abundant than the physical world we can observe with our eyes and through the world's most modern telescopes. "Yes," he will tell us, "my unbroken love is out there, undetectable through electromagnetic radiation but felt in every human heart." God will lean back on his throne, yawn, and check his fingernails as he says, "Oh ye of little minds. Wait, just wait until you join me in heaven. What a treat of knowledge and understanding I have for you! Yet, what I have chosen to share while you walk the earth is my love, for in my love, you have everything you need."

God knows what we truly need from him. He is there from infinity. He is without beginning or end. The idea of no starting place and no final conclusion challenges our ability to visualize and understand God, but he truly exudes an endless, unbounded reality. While we are encased in our meager reality of matter and energy and trapped in the four dimensions of length, width, height, and time, we will never truly understand the fundamental nature of God. We will never fully grasp the relationship between the physical world and our perception of God's position in it.

So, let's break our verse down into three revealing, love-inspired concepts. "*The peace [love] of God...*" tells us that our Father is intensely, intimately connected to us as his creation and his children. "*Which transcends all understanding ...*" means he is in control of all that happens to us. He can and will manage our situation for our good. He "*will guard your hearts and your minds in Christ Jesus.*" God is our protector and champion.

We don't understand what drives his nurturing compassion, but we can be assured it's there. We might try to compare it to a parent's compelling love for a child, but we only scratch the surface. It's so much more. God's love is the dark matter the fills in the spaces in the world and the cosmos, the substance we can't see or touch but that cushions all creation with the divine and unbreakable love of the Lord.

To the Ends of the Earth

But you will receive power when the Holy Spirit comes on you; and you will be my witnesses in Jerusalem, and in all Judea and Samaria, and to the ends of the earth.

— Acts 1:8 —

Responsibility. The Great Commission. God as unfathomable dark matter filling in all the spaces between what we can see, touch, and hear.

Responsibility gives us the authority to act, the control to make things happen, the power to bring the necessary supplies and systems to bear, the leadership to provide motivation, and the influence that oils the machine that makes it all happen.

Yet, responsibility also layers on us the burden of duty, the liability for success, the need for trust, and the guilt if we can't follow through. Jesus said, "I send you unto all the nations, to the ends of the earth, to spread my gospel to all people." This is the Great Commission, his charge for all Christians, none excepted.

What is your place in the role of the Great Commission? What part does God expect you to play? In what way are you culpable, are you at fault, are you *liable* for spreading the Good News of God's love to the lost across the globe?

Our verse gives us our answer. *"But you will receive power when the Holy Spirit comes on you ..."*

This is the reason evangelicals place so much emphasis on the infilling of the Holy Spirit. It's from the Holy Spirit that we receive the ability, the endurance, and the power to travel to places where we might well face hardship and threats on our life in order to tell people of the love of God.

We know of St. Patrick's Day, wearing green and the shamrocks that represent the event each March.

But, do we know of his heart for evangelization, of leaving his life in Britain to preach the gospel in Ireland? He was abducted as a teen and enslaved in Ireland. He escaped and returned home, and with his deep, Christian faith, returned to the land of his abductors as a missionary. God's love as seen through St. Patrick's eyes transcended the borders of his country and the pain of his enslavement at the hands of his abductors.

All Christians know of St. Paul. Originally named Saul, once God got Paul's attention, Paul traveled extensively, established churches, and wrote much of what we know as the biblical New Testament. He did all this despite repeatedly being thrown in prison and abused for his faith. What inspired him? The unfailing love of God to all men.

Then there are the missionaries who have given all in their dedication to spread the love of God to those who do not believe on or know him. On the blog of the Evangelical Free Church of America (EFCA), we read of five men in 1956 who traveled to Ecuador to present the gospel of Jesus and share the love of God with the Auca Indians. Jim Elliot, the leader of the team, along with Nate Saint, Ed McCully, Peter

Fleming, and Roger Youderian left behind wives, children, homes, and jobs to carry the good news of the gospel with them to foreign lands. They embodied the ideals of the Great Commission in their actions as well as in their hearts. Tragically, on January 8 of that year, all five men were martyred as they strove to propagate the gospel to those who needed to hear the story of God's compassion and love the most. These five men felt the call to share the salvation message because of their love for mankind and their determination to follow in the footsteps of Our Lord as they took his command to heart.

Here's what's vital to glean from this story. These men's deaths didn't dampen the call of the Great Commission. Rather, it motivated others to step in the martyrs' shoes to continue the race they had begun. Jim's wife wrote two books containing the profound truths found in the words her husband penned while in service to God, touching many by the witness Jim exhibited during his lifetime.

God's love transcends every border, even the final one. From our yard to our neighbor's yard, from our city to the one down the road, to the state a day's drive away, God's love flows freely. From our church to those of other denominations, in this city or across the globe, there's no shortage of God's love. From cultures infused with Christianity to people who have never heard the name of Jesus, the upwelling of God's love draws all mankind to him.

You will be my witnesses to the ends of the earth.

Jesus calls, God provides, and it's up to us to engage our feet to preach the gospel to all men.

Even for the Enemy

Love your enemies and pray for those who persecute you.

— Matthew 5:44 —

Love for my enemies ... seriously, Jesus? Those with evil intent for my welfare, and you deem them worthy of my love?

This is a hard concept to grasp, especially for believers new to the Christian faith. We often picture people submitting to beatings while bleating, "I forgive you. I love you. I pray God's blessing upon you."

Is that truly what "love your enemies" is all about,

being the doormat for people who choose to strike at us so that they might feel strong and powerful in comparison? The life of Apostle Paul sheds light on what the Divine Teacher means in this directive, and yes, it is a directive, not an option.

Paul abused the fledgling Christian faith with the strong fist of determination and presumptuous self-righteousness. "Saul began ravaging the church, entering house after house, and he would drag away men and women and put them in prison" (Acts 8:3 NASB). Paul/Saul was THE enemy of the early Christians. I can imagine the early followers of the faith whispering to one another, "If you hear of Saul entering the city, RUN!" They weren't wrong, either.

Then came pushback from God, where he stopped Saul on the road to Damascus and wagged his finger at him, saying, "Why, Saul? Why pick on me?" In that moment, everything changed.

Did you get that? Saul hated the followers of Jesus which closely aligns with saying that Saul hated Jesus, or at least the idea of him. God loved him anyway. He didn't smack him aside the head, leave him in the ditch bleeding from his ears, and intone, "Touch my followers again and you'll get worse."

Rather, God saw the good that Saul could achieve if he could be loved into the kingdom. The proof of God's faith is strewn throughout the New Testament.

Once Paul became a messenger of the gospel, segments of both Jewish and gentile groups opposed him. Some Christians also saw him as divisive, the man who had been one thing and was now another. Could he be trusted, and anyway, what right did this interloper have to tell them what to believe and to do?

Are you seeing it? God's example to Paul to "love your enemies" was well learned. Did Paul dismiss those who sought his neck? No. He ministered to Jews who railed against him, the gentiles who wanted him out of the way, and even Christian factions who were polluting the message of Jesus to benefit themselves. Paul sought out those from various backgrounds, who many times were his "enemies" who rejected his message, even as Paul struggled to prove himself a dedicated adherent to the Christian faith.

The Jewish leaders, especially, were constantly at odds with Paul. He had been on their side and now he wasn't. This led Paul to focus his ministry on non-Jewish people. Even in these groups outside the Jewish faith, some were especially resistant to Paul's teaching, including the Judaizers, who were Jewish Christians who believed gentiles who found faith in Jesus must follow Jewish law, and the Gnostics who focused on esoteric, possibly even occult knowledge and dualism, in which salvation comes through knowledge and not faith.

Despite his frequent opposition, Paul lived out Matthew 5:44. He taught the early Christians to love their enemies and treat them with kindness. And remember, this was before the New Testament was assembled, before the church had the gospel of Mark for instruction, and before the centuries of canon that today grounds many modern Christians in their faith, beliefs, and actions.

Through Paul's example, we are given only one option. We must actively connect with and minister to even our enemies. When someone rejects the message of Jesus (or even us as his emissary), we must demonstrate forgiveness. In doing so, people will see through our actions the transformative power of God's love. We will be the hand of God reaching out to shower his love on them, for in our love and compassion, God is revealed in his divine majesty.

There Is No "Too Far"

Where can I go from your Spirit?

— Psalm 139:7 —

David is considered the ultimate choir leader, the master of the music, the man who can put his heart and emotions into words and create a connection with us that extends over the millennia. Psalm 139 begins with, "You have searched for me, Lord, and you know me" (v. 1). Then David describes all the places he might possibly try to hide and why in each one, his attempts to run from God are completely pointless.

David says:

"If I reach the heavens ..."

"If I travel to the depths of the oceans ..."

"If I rise at the dawn ... or make my way to the far side of the sea ..."

"Even when I cower in the darkness ... I am not hidden from the Lord."

Then, David describes God's enduring presence:

"You are there ... your hand will guide me ... the night will shine like day because you are there."

As children, the story of Jonah is fascinating. To be *swallowed* ... by a *fish* ... and shivers run down our spines. Yet, the glory of the story isn't Jonah being swallowed by the fish but the fact that God was there with him. Jonah did everything he could think of to run from God, to hide himself from the Almighty, to disappear from the duties handed to him directly from God.

And God said, "Not yet, Jonah. I'm not letting you off so easily. I've still got work for you to do." Then God said, "Let's get out of here and make our way to Ninevah to complete the task at hand."

This story is ultimately about God's love reaching into the depths of the ocean to pull a man from the morass of misguided self-righteousness he'd wallowed in for far too long.

Towards the end of this psalm (or song) of David, we see part of the reason for his desire for reconnection with God. Verses 19-20 say, "If only you, God, would slay the wicked! Away from me, you who are bloodthirsty! They speak of you with evil intent; your adversaries misuse your name."

As with Jonah, David feels the world folding in on him. He desperately needs to know that God is reaching out to him, that he is more than a speck upon the earth who had been forgotten by his maker.

We can easily fall into David's trap, so similar to Jonah and others in the Bible who lost sight of the awesome and consuming presence of God that fills every available space around us.

Moses hid in Midian, hoping to never be found by the Egyptians or by God.

Cain hoped desperately to hide his murder of his brother, Abel, from the Lord.

Even Adam and Eve hid from God once they had eaten of the Tree of the Knowledge of Good and Evil.

The prophet Elijah once abandoned the world for a cave, hoping to hide from his problems—and likely from God. I Kings 19:9 in the NLT shows us God's response: "There [Elijah] came to a cave, where he spent the night. But the LORD said to him, 'What are you doing here, Elijah?'"

That's what God says to us when we try to hide from him. *What are you doing here? Why aren't you out doing my work? I have a plan for you, and it's not hiding in the depths of a dark cave.*

Whatever we've done, whatever the weight we carry, however bad it seems to us, God is at our side.

We can never do something so bad, run so far, ignore him so often that he waves us away and says, "Okay, if this is what you want, have at it." Instead, he comes to us with faith that we can listen to him, make the right choices, and return unto him. Each time he approaches us, his question to us is always the same.

"What are you doing here?"

Then he says, "Take my hand, and together let's return into the light, rediscover your life, and rest in my protection. Your future is just beginning to unfold, and I will be there with you."

— 5 —

Love That Transforms

Becoming Who You Were
Created to Be

We love because He first loved us.

— I John 4:19 —

Nicky Cruz is an example of love that transforms people into the person God intends for them to be. Apolonio Garcia is another. God took him from prison to the pulpit. Then there's the Apostle Paul, one of the most dramatic transformations in written history. God cast him to the ground on the road to

Damascus, and Paul stood up again, forever changed by God's love.

Other biblical characters who were completely and irrevocably changed by God's love include Zacchaeus, the tax collector; all twelve disciples, who changed from fishermen to fishers of men; Rahab, from prostitute to protector of the spies; Sampson, who killed more of the enemy upon his death than in all his life; the Prodigal Son; Jonah; Nicodemus; even Moses, from frightened refugee to Pharoah's worst nightmare.

God's love can also change us in smaller ways. Our child is born, and through the realization of God's love, we abandon our youthful, party-filled ways. Or God rescues us from a cascading catastrophe of bad choices, and we choose to rededicate our life to him. Through these life-changing moments, we learn more and more of the depths of God's love for his creation. We learn to trust in him and place our lives in his hands. We choose to allow ourselves to become the person God created us to be—kinder, softer spoken, gentle with the hurting, and attuned to the leading of the Lord. We choose to display the love of the Lord to others because of his love toward us.

The Power of Being Known and Loved

Whoever loves God is known by God.

— I Corinthians 8:3 —

Let's look first at one of the most poignant interactions with Jesus that reveals how being recognized by Our Lord can dramatically change a person's direction forever.

Let's set the scene, although it's one you will easily recognize. We've endured a trial, although the charges were blatantly manufactured. Sentence has been passed, and the victim has been whipped roundly with a device that is manufactured in such a way that it pulls the skin from their back in a gruesome manner.

You know this story, right? Even without being told the name of the victim, you already have enough clues. Going on, we reveal the cross, the man alongside the road who is forced to help carry it, nails through the hands and feet … the trauma is inescapable.

However, although you know this is about Jesus, it's not Jesus that's the point of this example. It's one of the men being crucified at his side. The man asks nothing from Jesus except to be remembered when he comes into his kingdom.

Here's where love comes into the picture.

Jesus, while wrapped in a haze of pain and suffering, steps outside of his agony and takes the time to notice the thief at his side. He hears the man's words, and Jesus changes the ending of the man's life. Jesus says simply, "Today you will be with me in paradise" (Luke 23:43).

Being known. Being loved. An existence changed forever.

Children who are ignored by busy parents often turn into rowdy teens who get into frequent trouble that requires their parents to deal with their misbehaviors. Even bad attention can be better than no attention at all. We need our presence recognized, our attendance checked off and validated, our contribution to what's at hand stamped with "I noticed you!" If we are validated with love, that's best. If it takes the rod, then we at least know we are real and are making an impact, even if it's a negative one.

You may recognize the name of Macauley Culkin, the boy from the *Home Alone* films. At age 16, he essentially divorced his parents. He was wildly loved by his fans but felt abandoned by those who should have been closest to him.

Another entertainment icon, Drew Barrymore, most notably seen in *E.T. the Extra-Terrestrial* as a young girl, sought emancipation at an even younger age. At 15, Barrymore said, "Enough! I don't need you any longer."

On the opposite side of the angst coin, screen great Chris Hemsworth stepped back from acting because of his love for his family. He is quoted as saying: "I've got three kids who I want to spend more time with."

Hollywood royalty Cary Grant shifted from his role as an acclaimed actor to stay-at-home dad when his daughter was born in 1966. His daughter, Jennifer, says, "Dad didn't think acting and having a family went hand in hand."

John 3:16 is one of Christendom's most iconic verses. "For God so loved the world ..." God didn't say, "Enough! I don't need you any longer!" Rather, he said, "I've got children I want to spend more time with." God looked upon the earth, saw what humanity was dealing with, and his heart was moved. In his love, he said, "Having a family and forgiveness go hand in hand. I accept the challenge and opportunity to love and care for my children. They are mine, and I will envelop them with my love."

When we respond back, when we accept the calling of the Christ, when our heart is filled with love for our Creator, God's heart is warmed, and he floods our life with ever-greater levels of his peace, joy, and love.

In essence, when we reveal our love for him, his love flows back unto us.

Grace that Shapes You

The grace of God ... teaches us to say "No"
to ungodliness ... and to live self-controlled,
upright and godly lives.

— Titus 2:11-12 —

Transformation. It means to be one thing and then to become another. Ice becomes water which turns into vapor. Carbon becomes trees which we can turn into heat by fire. Petroleum becomes fuel and plastics and clothing and appliances.

It's one thing, then another, often so different that we can hardly recognize where it began. This is what grace does to us when we choose to commit ourselves to the full, unadulterated love of God.

You may have heard of Mike Lindell or seen him in his popular commercials for the pillow company MyPillow. Mike says this: "I was a very functioning cocaine addict." He shared on a Pure Flix podcast that he was freed from his cocaine addiction in 2009 but surrendered fully to Jesus in 2017. God chased him and made him a new man.

You may not have heard of Olympian Louis Zamperini. His son, Luke, tells of his father as a WWII veteran and prisoner of war. He was a "punk kid" who made it to the Olympics before joining the military. He survived for 47 days at sea before being picked up by the Japanese and put into a prison camp. After returning home, he accepted Jesus at a Billy Graham revival and found forgiveness for the prison guards who tortured him in the Japanese prison. Grace transformed Louis Zamperini's life from that point forward, and he became a new man.

How about musician Jen Ledger? Today, she belongs to the Christian rock band Skillet, but that isn't who she once was. To her, all believers were little more than hypocrites. However, her brother's life intersected with Christianity and started her on a discovery of the love of God and his divine mercy.

Bryan Flanery was deployed to Afghanistan with the U.S. Army where physical and emotional scars forced him to the edge. Desperate, he swallowed two bottles of pills, but God had another plan. An encounter with God took him along a path leading to the revelation of God's mercy, grace, and love. He was changed from teetering off a cliff to embracing life.

Casey Diaz spent his teenage years in and out of prison. He dodged capture at 16 after committing murder. Three weeks later, he was in custody of the Los Angeles Police Department. During his time in prison, Jesus intervened in Diaz's life, and he is now a pastor who shares the love of God with his congregation.

Even those who lead respectable, enviable lifestyles can struggle with darkness. Pastor and author Ben Courson suffered from chronic depression for a decade. It took away his motivation to continue, and ending it all seemed the only way. Yet, God's hand of love and compassion intervened. While Courson desired (and tried) to end his life, God had a better plan. The love of Jesus won out. Courson says via the Pure Flix podcast, "Psalm 37:4 [says] … you will overcome your nightmares because of your dreams … You can overcome anything."

Bad to good. *Or just wrestling with life and getting a grip.* God's love can change us as we are shaped and renewed through his grace in five steps of divine transformation.

One, we must repent and accept forgiveness. It's free and for everyone, but we must accept it.

Two, we must delve into the Bible and learn of the ways of God. Only then can we discern what is of God and what is of the world.

Three, we must step away from our old ways. We must say no to our past and to ungodliness. We are made new in Jesus (2 Cor. 5:17) and must live like it.

Four, we embrace different lives. The places we go, the friends we enjoy, even our levels of generosity and grace toward others. We will not be the same but will choose to put God's will at the top of our list.

Five, true sorrow for our past deeds and a vibrant and heartfelt repentance will align us with the ongoing will of God in our lives.

God has removed our transgressions from us (Ps. 103:12), and his kindness is intended to lead us to repentance (Rom. 2:4). His love shapes us into what he intends for us to become.

From Orphan to Heir

The Spirit you received brought about your adoption to sonship.

— Romans 8:15 —

Adoption, a benefit or a curse? A recent blog post from Australia tells the story of a 33-year-old woman whose older brother received government paperwork about his "adoption" 35 years earlier. After contacting the government agency to let them know of their mistake, as they were both certain it was an error and the correct recipient needed to be notified, the two visited their mother to let her know what had transpired.

When they walked in and mentioned the "adoption," the mother's face turned pale, and they knew the truth. The woman's older brother was adopted, and he never knew. The kicker was when the mother said to her daughter, "I have something to tell you, also."

It turned out that all adoptions at the time were closed. Their younger brother was born only after the eldest two were adopted, and their father hadn't wanted to differentiate between the three. After struggling with the news for a time, the blogger says she came to realize that they were all three loved so much that none of them had been able to tell who was adopted and who wasn't.

Adoption into sonship. That's our legacy as sons and daughters of the almighty God. We are loved so much that no one can tell who's the natural-born child and who's adopted into the family. We become part of the church, a safe and loving home, unlike where we previously experienced instability and hardship. God provides resources and opportunities to grow in his love and under his protection. He becomes our financial consultant, our health provider, and our extracurricular activities director. When we become part of his family, we know we are loved, and through his enveloping arms, our sense of identity as his child binds us tighter to our fellow believers.

In one way, our adoption is different from the siblings in Australia, as the body of Christ is open adoption all the way. We know we are adopted, even as we luxuriate in the ultimate love of our Father; but we can also reach out to our natural family as witnesses for Christ. We gain a sense of continuity in being part of God's family, all the while sharing the divine redemption we have received with our natural family. God's love bridges the gap.

Once we transition from the jumbled natural world and accept our new place in our adoptive spiritual family, we also gain improved health and well-being. Following the precepts taught in the Bible offers us longer life and a higher quality of relationships than trying to do it on our own. God has watched over his children for thousands of years, and when we educate ourselves by studying the truths in the Bible, we find that our lives will align with his teachings, bringing positive social and emotional development. We can even enjoy financial gain through biblical giving and investing practices, all available to us as adopted sons and daughters of God.

All that's in this life, but what about the next? Remember, when we receive salvation, we are adopted into the body of Christ. We are no longer on the outside. We have entered the sacred realm, moving from spiritual darkness to being in the light where there is no darkness at all.

As adoptees, we receive Jesus' promise of eternal life. He assured the thief on the cross that they would be together on the other side. It's the same promise he holds out to each of us. Our sins are forgiven, and we are now reconciled with God, resulting in a personal and intimate relationship with the supreme being of all time. Our new identity becomes that of Christian, believer, and son/daughter. We develop a new sense of self-worth and purpose that is watered and fertilized by the Father's love for each of us.

God's adoption of each of us gives us peace and reassurance that we are loved; guidance and wisdom in our life decisions; community and support by fellow believers; purpose and meaning though our place in God's plan; and greater compassion and love for those both in and out of the circle of believers.

Who wouldn't want to become an heir of the almighty God through salvation and the working of the Holy Spirit within us?

Let Love Lead

For Christ's love compels us ...

— 2 Corinthians 5:14 —

There's more to this verse, of course, about the sacrifice of Jesus—*who died for all of us*—and the connection his sacrifice creates for us in God's plan for humanity. We are compelled to follow in the footsteps of Jesus by his very example on the cross. He loved us—*and still loves us*—so much that our hearts prompt us in a duty-bound fashion to reflect that love back to those who walk this life with us.

Jesus is of course our finest and premier example of reflecting love to those around us. He healed people even when the authorities bucked the process (at the pool of Bethesda, Jn. 5:1-18) and spent time with the outcast (healing the lepers, Luke 5:12-16). We can also see this in the lives of missionaries who display the love of God and exemplify the example of Jesus through sacrificing their comfort, relationships, and sometimes their lives.

Three hundred years ago, Count Ludwig von

Zinzendorf was head of his class at the University of Wittenburg in Germany. While still in school, he started a twenty-four-hour prayer vigil that emboldened the Moravian Mission Society to send out more missionaries over the next two decades than the Protestants and Anglicans had sent in the previous two centuries.

We know of John Wesley. He was the son of a minister but started at Oxford University in 1720 as an unbeliever. He had several hiccups on his journey to missionary-hood, but a life-changing meeting with a Morovian missionary while returning from a failed missionary trip to the North American continent brought him assurance of his salvation. Wesley's achievements over his lifetime include setting the foundational precepts for the Methodist Church, traveling a quarter-million miles, and preaching 40,000 sermons. He also gave away ninety percent of his income.

In the 1880s, in England, a group of college students known as "The Cambridge Seven" jumpstarted the most effective missionary movement of all time. Two of the seven were notable athletes and two were military officers; and as a group, they inspired hundreds of people to volunteer for the China Inland Missionary Agency (CIM). They set sail for China in 1885, and by the time they arrived, CIM had gained 163 missionaries. By 1900, CIM represented fully a third of all the Protestant missionaries in China.

Just after The Cambridge Seven set off for China, Luther Wishard in the United States invited internationally known minster D.L. Moody to Massachusetts to speak at the Mt. Hermon Conference grounds to 252 college men from 89 U.S. colleges. Wishard, Moody, and a Princeton senior, Robert Wilder, ignited the crowd, and by the end of the conference, 100 of the men had signed a declaration to "go to the unevangelized portions of the world" and became known as "The Mt. Hermon 100." Eventually, more than 100,000 students became involved, with 20,000 going overseas and the rest forming the Laymen's Missionary Movement to provide at-home support for the traveling missionaries.

Grace Wilder, Robert's older sister, asked the question: "Can we not enlist every one of the 600 schools where young women are educated, so that united we may undertake our work, that of carrying the gospel into every nation?" To support her dedication to her cause, she sailed at age 26 for India to immerse herself in sharing the gospel story with the subcontinent. She chose to give her life to mobilizing college students and evangelizing the world.

While not everyone can travel to distant lands to speak of the love of Christ to those who are unfamiliar with the message of Jesus, those of us at home can support those with the call to dedicate themselves to God's work in foreign lands through donations, volunteering our time, and raising awareness of their needs.

Jesus' example on the cross and the love he revealed through his sacrifice compels us to involve ourselves in The Great Commission to go unto all the world to spread the Good News of Christ.

Made to Reflect His Heart

Everyone who loves has been born of God
and knows God.

— I John 4:7 —

God's heart is filled with love for his creation. When he fills us up, that love begins to overflow onto those around us. We become a "home missionary" both in our physical homes as well as in the world in which we exist. Our jobs, the extracurricular activities that take up our evenings and weekends, and our family time all count as our personal missionary time. How we treat others during each of these times reveals our faith and values. This is not just for church, on Sundays, or when someone's watching. Our everyday life must be filled with love and compassion as a positive example of Christ living through us.

Our daily walk and positive example are our opportunity to let the love of God flow from our heart to those at our side. How can we become home missionaries? By sharing our faith, serving others, and finding ways to volunteer and serve our community. Here's some suggestions that will make your Christian life shine:

Daily prayer is your foundation to receiving God's guidance. When you speak to God and *allow time for him to speak to you,* you will discover wisdom that applies to all areas of your life.

Look around you for people in need. The love and

compassion you show to them will become their network of support. Ask how you can help and then *do it.*

Tell others the story of your walk with God. Hearing of your faith and how it impacts your life will resonate with those who are drawn to the faith.

Get into a local church. Actively participate by volunteering in areas that interest you. When the opportunity arises, contribute your resources, whether it is time or money.

Steer your conversations with others to your faith and why you believe as you do. Be open about who you are in Christ and how he has impacted your life. Give them a chance to ask questions and respond with respect and kindness.

Invite visitors to your church out for lunch. A warm welcome will do more to draw them to Christ than preaching ever will. While at lunch, center your conversation on your church, your beliefs, and how they might benefit from your church fellowship.

Participate in church activities, and not just the "three-times-a-week services." You build relationships through shared activities. Plan a group camping trip to a local overnight park. Visit the state fair. A backyard barbecue ... trip to the lake ... women's day out ... men's golf tournament ... the options are endless.

Determine which church causes align with God's leading for you. You can't support everything, but you can support something. Then, give generously. Even financial support for outside charities will reflect the love of Jesus to those who receive your support.

Apply kingdom values to every part of your life. The 1896 book *In His Steps* by Charles Sheldon asks a question that redirects every part of every day with this question: *What would Jesus do?* When we ask ourselves this, it changes our outlook on so many things.

That annoying panhandler just outside the supermarket ... what would Jesus do?

Our sister, once again needing money to cover her mortgage ... what would Jesus do?

Our children running amok at school ... what would Jesus do?

Our business partner siphoning money from the company accounts ... what would Jesus do?

This simple question creates a whirlwind of self-searching thought that makes us consider each action we take and how it impacts our witness for Christ. Does it show the love of Jesus to those who receive the output of our actions? Or do they walk away from us feeling downcast and unappreciated?

God is filled with love for his creation. He expects us to reflect that love in how we live each day.

— 6 —

Love on Display

Loving Others as We've Been Loved

By this everyone will know that you are My disciples, if you love one another.

— John 13:35 —

Love hidden isn't love at all.

It's well known that abusive behaviors in families are generational. What mama does is how her daughter treats her children. The example learned from the father is exactly how the son parents his little ones.

How is the same not true for the love Jesus expects us to share with others? In the church, if we welcome strangers, no matter how strange, our children will learn to welcome them also. Ratty hair. Inappropriate clothing. Maybe they pray too loudly ... whatever we don't see as "Sunday morning behavior" is either discounted and dismissed *or we choose to overlook it and love them into our fellowship.*

Jesus fellowshipped with sinners. Even the disciples were a rough group of fishermen, likely smelly, with poorly tended fingernails and ragged beards. Then there's Zacchaeus, the tax collector. The tax collectors of the day were seen as Roman collaborators and traitors to the Jewish people and ... drum roll ... Jesus chatted them up like his best friends.

And oh, mercy me! The *prostitutes.* Jesus engaged with them as he demonstrated his willingness to reach out to the disenfranchised of his day. He also reached out to groups like the Samaritans, as seen in the story of the Samaritan woman at the well.

There are other recorded interactions with a Roman Centurion, a Canaanite woman, and lepers. His goal was to set an example for his disciples and followers, and through the stories in the Bible, to modern-day Christians. What is that example? Because Jesus loved those most in need, we are to do the same.

Love Is the Mission

The entire law is fulfilled in keeping this one command: "Love your neighbor as yourself."

— Galatians 5:14 —

Who is our neighbor? Who are we commanded to love? Where do we draw the line between loving this person, but that person is too distant from our life (lifestyle, social position, or physical location) to be our responsibility?

John 13:34-35 tells us, "A new command I give you: Love one another. As I have loved you, so you must love one another. By this everyone will know that you are my disciples, if you love one another."

These are the words of Jesus, so one of the ways we can determine the limits of our love responsibility is to study the life of Jesus. Who did he love? Where did he find these people? How far did he consider too far to reach out to them?

Matthew 22:39 reiterates our verse in Galatians, telling us: "Love your neighbor as yourself." I Peter 22:39 encourages us to display "unity of mind, sympathy, brotherly love, a tender heart, and a humble mind." Even John 15:12 steps up with: "A new command is this: Love each other as I have loved you," restating a similar verse from two chapters earlier.

We can learn a lesson here. Say it once to make your point. Say it twice to send it home, meaning this truth is vital in the teachings of Our Lord.

Who can do this, and by this, I mean to love all people as Jesus did? He attended dinner parties with saboteurs to the Jewish faith (tax collectors), met up with socially inappropriate people in out-of-the-way places (the woman at the well), and didn't heed social distancing when faced with disease (the lepers).

Philippians 4:13 motivates us: "I can do all things through Christ who strengthens me." All things! Our neighbor who complains about the length of our grass? God says we can show them love despite their poor attitude. The boss who overlooked us for the promotion we desired and hired someone younger and better looking? Yes, the love Jesus instills into us can and will overflow onto them. Our brother who stole our identity and bought a new truck *that he didn't even make the payments on?* That's a tough one, but yes, God's love stretches to cover even that.

We read in John 13:35: "By this everyone will know that you are my disciples, if you love one another." Sure, that neighbor might be like a rash that keeps coming back, but God's love is a soothing ointment. When you show them love, you become Christ to them.

That boss? They may not notice the love of Christ in your actions, but your coworkers will. Your love will reflect all over them, and they will know you are a person of God who stands by the principles of the Word.

Your brother is harder. The tie of family binds you together, while the familiarity of past abuses trips your switch into overdrive before you can say goodness me. Yet we read in Proverbs 17:17 that "a friend loves at all times, and a brother is born for a time of adversity." Bibleref.com explains that if we act as a genuine brother, we are there during unfavorable (and abusive) circumstances as well as in the good times.

For our friends, it is easy to sacrifice, but we must be willing to do even more for a brother.

Let's pull this together with two final verses. The first is found in Colossians 3:14: "And above all these, put on love, which is the perfect bond of unity." The place or condition or offense or relationship is of less importance than the love we choose to display. When we practice love, God uses our actions to draw others unto him.

The second verse is Romans 8:28, which most of us will recognize: "And we know that all things work together for good to those who love God, to those who are called according to his purpose." No matter how difficult it is to show love to the unlovable, God can use us in every circumstance to reveal his love to those who need it most.

Seeing the Image of God in Others

So God created mankind in His own image . . .

— Genesis 1:27 —

Behavior or birthright? What do we see when we look at other people, their actions or the image of the God that created them?

If we see only the actions of fallen man, then who can claim to be the son or daughter of God? We are in a broken state, even as children of God. We will stumble and occasionally fall into the muck of this world. God must lift us out of the mire and clean us off so that we can shine with his goodness once again.

So, what do we hope people see, the muck we stumbled into or the cleaning that God is doing on us? Judy Corridon addresses this question in a Quora post as she recounts being on the subway when several inebriated men on the way home from work joined her and her husband. They were very disorderly, and her first response was to dismiss them as trouble-makers and the prelude to an unpleasant journey until she and her husband could exit at their stop.

Then her thoughts shifted to her available choices. She could see them as an intrusion into her day or as God's creation, formed in the likeness of the Savior. From that point, Judy says that she felt the impending turmoil replaced by the presence of God, and she was surrounded by peace and harmony for the remainder of the journey.

Here's what we can take from this: It isn't just the preacher who's created in the image of God. Not just the church soloist, the missionary in a distant land, or the Sunday school worker who labors each Saturday evening to prepare the lesson. The homeless person on the church steps … the driver who cut you off in traffic … the waitress who forgot your second cup of coffee … we are all created in the image of God. Our arms, legs, brain … and the spirit that lives inside us. We are 100-percent formed, molded, and imprinted with his nature, fully equipped to commune with him, no matter how we choose to live our lives. We only need the desire and the opportunity to shift our goals from us to Christ.

The truth is that most people are searching for something more, to experience a "God-moment" in their lives. In a study group of over-55 Baby Boomers, the leader asked this question: When is a time you experienced God in your life? Hands went up, and the answers flowed: "At sixteen, I was with friends …"; "When I was 27, I felt the move of God …"; "Several years ago, during answered prayer …".

The leader of the group was taken aback that the

group seemed to have missed his point. He had expected people to say, "Yesterday, God showed me …" or, "This morning, God revealed …".

The leader of the group stressed that our God-moments should happen every day, and they likely do. We just don't focus on them, and we let them slip away. Here's our takeaway: If we can't see what God is doing in our lives, how can we find him in others? Just as the momentous touch of God slips by unnoticed in our life, buried in the hustle and bustle, so it happens with those we interact with.

Our solution is to choose to see God through the disruption, the alcohol, or while traveling alongside people who make us uncomfortable. If Fred humiliates us in front of the office crew, we can choose to call him self-centered or honor him as God's creation. We must surrender our dislike (or even hatred) and choose to forgive. We must ask, "What if Fred was given the opportunity to experience God's mercy and forgiveness? What would Fred be like then?"

The resolution may not be Fred coming to a saving knowledge of Jesus but rather the change in our heart and attitude when we view Fred as being created in the image of God. We need to allow the truth of the Bible to help us see others through God's eyes.

When It Costs You Something

He took out two denarii and gave them to the innkeeper ...

— Luke 10:35 —

A denarius (singular form) is an unfamiliar monetary term, meaning we may recognize the word but have no equivalent to compare it to. As in, what could we purchase with it? Will it make the house payment, buy a run of groceries, or gas up the car?

In Matthew 20:2, we read that a landowner agrees to pay his workers a day's wage, or one denarius. Now we can place a value on a denarius. We can determine how much we are paid for a day's work and equate it to that.

So let's look back to our verse in Luke. Two days' wages to help a random stranger. How much is that for you? $50? $100? $250? Or perhaps we can use this parable to equate giving of ourselves in other ways to determine just what it costs us when we follow

Jesus. With this new direction in mind, let's look at the personal cost of being a Christian, of sharing the love of God with the world, and see how that compares with God's love for us.

The world says, "Me first!" Let me care for my own needs, and then I will share what I have left over. That includes material possessions (Donate your gently used vehicle to Cars for Christ!), social status (Hang out with the homeless at our Wednesday Night Food Pantry!), or career opportunities (Volunteer for Doctors Across Borders today!).

The needs of others must take priority over ours. As a Christian, we must focus on the things and opportunities that align with our Christian values and fully commit. That bespoke coffee on the way to work? Moving up to a finer automobile? That new pool? Yes ... er, apologies, God ... NO! I will choose to provide for those with greater needs than mine.

What about when we don't get invites because we don't party acceptably? Our faith makes us a wet blanket on good times, and we're not welcomed to the "rowdier side of life." Or we get "faith-bashed" by liberals who disagree with our conservative values? Our Christian witness becomes a struggle to maintain.

Then there's our mandate from Jesus to go into all the world to share the gospel message. Perhaps a mission trip between college and our first job … giving up our Saturdays to help the elderly in the church … teaching a Sunday school class, taking church membership classes, attending yet another Bible study, or serving on the church board. Each of these requires time, energy, and a commitment to help others.

We also must consider the direct financial cost. We are encouraged to invest in things eternal rather than in material possessions we cannot take with us. Donate to the church building fund. Give your tithes, then extra offerings at every request. What good is money in the bank when your soul is stained with greed? There's truth to all of this, but we are also giving up what we can enjoy today for a benefit that only comes when we move on from this life. We open our wallet now for the purpose of rewards in the afterlife.

Yet all is not lost! Our Christian walk costs us something, but it's not all bad! Let's look at four things we give up that benefit us every day.

First, we throw away self-righteousness. We no

longer have to be the one to chart our own journey to heaven. We no longer need to tally our church attendance, the prayers we say, or the coins we drop in the offering plate. Those are not what connect us to Christ.

We also kick sin out the door. We abandon our bad habits and let them fade away. No truces with sin are allowed, and we endeavor to remain clean and pure before God. We learn to walk after the example of Jesus.

Then, we pull up our boots and get busy for Jesus. We stand on guard in private as well as in public. We refuse to let others slide, remain in need, or suffer unnecessarily. Our outlook becomes Christ for all and all for Christ.

And finally, we become content with God's approval. Let the world disagree and even mock our faith, for if God is pleased, then no other opinion matters. In Noah's day, mankind mocked Noah for his faith in the instructions of God, but when the waters of tribulation rose, only the ones who placed their contentment in the approval of God survived the deluge.

It costs to be a Christian. We give up much, but

we gain so much more!

Love Speaks Truth with Grace

*Speaking the truth in love, we will grow to
become in every respect the mature body of
him who is the head, that is, Christ.*

— Ephesians 4:15 —

God's perfect love is a mighty force, a tsunami that sweeps aside everything in its way. And just like a tsunami, we must be careful how we apply it. If we use God's love to batter relentlessly at those who resist the plan of God, it will undercut every good intention. It will become a wall of roiling force digging out the foundations of good will that God has begun in them. Instead, we must aim the truth of redemption (and sometimes correction) with the gentle hand of God's compassion so that when the tsunami has passed by, those we are trying to reach remain firmly rooted in the truth God desires for us to share.

How do we corner the market on God's grace, on the compassion of the Father, and on the tender touch of the Holy Spirit? How do we fashion a jewel out of our desire to stamp the truth of God onto the lives of everyone around us? Let's look at five facets of our grace stone, the sparkling jewel of compassion and truth that shimmers with the love that flows endlessly from God's heart through our lips and our actions, and onto those who need to hear it most.

We begin by seeking God's Word. We look for passages that back up God's message of love without battering the unsaved with burdensome rules and regulations. There are rules, yes, and regulations are there to protect us in the faith, but they are aids to success rather than bludgeons to make the needy bleed.

A good second step is to make prayer a consistent part of our daily life. Schedule it in and *stick to the schedule.* The length of the prayer time you choose to set aside is less important than consistency. Tell God you'll be there and then show up. You can separate your time with God into sessions for guidance, strength, or discernment. With the Word at your side, God can (and will) direct you to specific scriptures to clarify his will in your life.

We cannot forget that grace is never far from

community, for community is the sandpaper that wears away the rough edges of life. So, join a prayer group. Invite your Sunday school class to the lake for the day. Have a backyard barbecue ... and talk about things of the Lord. Share your spiritual progress. Learn to trust one another as you practice grace through sharing the ups and downs of your spiritual walk.

The book of I Samuel tells us it is better to obey God's directives than to sacrifice our time, possessions, and desires (v. 15:22). If we give up what we possess and refuse to follow God's revealed plan for our life, what hope is there for us? This passage goes on to say that if we refuse to accept *and follow* God's will, it's the same as witchcraft (v. 23, KJV). So, even when it is a challenge, strive to accept the plan God has revealed for your life as found in the Bible and DO IT each day, every day, and even the day after that.

Our final step in learning to live in grace is to find a position in which to serve others, especially within the church or in your community. Pick up the pastor's car each Saturday and run it through the car wash. Ask if there's a food pantry that can use your help. Teach a Sunday class (or even the teen boys on Wednesday night). Host a Bible study, either at your church or in your home. When you begin to serve others, you will grow in grace. When you accept the responsibility to do the good that God's open doors provide, you will both demonstrate your love for God and learn how to speak God's truth with the grace that it deserves.

The Church as a Living Love Letter

You are a letter from Christ ... written not with ink but with the Spirit ...

— 2 Corinthians 3:3 —

God's perfect love lived out through our actions serves as a powerful testimony and witness to the communities in which we live. As an individual, we can touch those at our side, those who live and work with us daily, and sometimes the people we interact with on a random basis. If we can do so much individually, how much more can we accomplish for the Lord when we team up with other believers to promote and act out the love of God? Is there a group out there for like believers, for people who want to band together to step out for Christ?

Yes! And you're likely already involved in it. It's called the CHURCH!

You are directly commissioned by Christ to go into the world and present the gospel to all people. That's a personal directive known in the religious world as The Great Commission. Just like the example of wrapping your fingers with thread, where one is easily broken, but wrap it a hundred times, and the weakest of threads has you firmly bound. Individually, we may struggle to reach the lost with God's love, but put a hundred of us together, and there's no stopping what we can do!

Sharing God's love is more than just about bashing the broken with the salvation message. As Jesus said in Matthew 14:16 when the disciples suggested sending the hungry crowds to find their own food, "You feed them." Here are ways we can "feed" our communities, ways we can live out the love of God to those around us.

The church can become a central player in organizing concerts, festivals, and fairs. Think Christmas pageants, Fall Fun Festivals, Mother's Day outings, or

Father-Daughter banquets. We will build connections between the church and the community.

We can focus on youth through sports events, the arts, and educational opportunities. We all know about Vacation Bible Schools, but up the game. Start a church league and invite the public to join. There are Bible versions of spelling bees and trivia challenges. All are ripe for church appropriation.

What about volunteer initiatives? Assign someone to a table in the foyer with a sign-up list for local charities, hospitals, and schools. These organizations need all the help they can get, and you will interweave God's mission into the time you spend with each group.

The church can also impact the community through environmental stewardship. Establish a community-wide clean-up drive overseen by the church. See what's already available, then target overlooked needs, such as clearing a creek or roadside of excess debris. Passersby will see your church's involvement and experience God's love in action.

Additional ways to be a living love letter to your community are to connect with local non-profit organizations; leverage the skills within your church body to offer free clinics, musical performances, or even healthy eating workshops; deliver food to the elderly or to homeless shelters; offer after-school tutoring or free English classes for adults; provide daycare for struggling parents or support to families with special-needs children; and finally, engage in random (i.e., intentional and planned) acts of kindness such as visiting the sick or practical assistance like yard trimming or snow removal.

Love can be an emotional thing, which is how our society presents it through the entertainment media. Yet, if we leave it there, we've skipped over so many love opportunities that we may as well not have bothered. Yes, showing love will give us emotional rewards, but it's the action of love that matters to the unloved. A hungry child won't feel loved if we hug them without feeding them. A lonely senior will experience more love from a morning of snow removal than they ever will from a televangelist on a TV screen.

We, as the church, are God's living love letter to our community.

— 7 —

Love That Never Ends

Living in Eternal Relationship with God

And now these three remain: faith, hope and love. But the greatest of these is love.

— I Corinthians 13:13 —

Love, the romantic sort.

We've heard the statistics. In the U.S.A., 41 percent of first-time marriages end in divorce, with the percentages climbing closer to 50 percent for all marriages. Over 115 studies suggest that divorce rates are trending downward, but martial separations have expanded to fill the gap. Essentially, American families are being fractured down the middle.

So, what happened to the love? When did the romance fade? These are very real questions we must ask, because the next one is whether everyone is going to leave us in the end. We crave a sure thing, someone who won't abandon us, a relationship that provides a firm footing to embolden us as we challenge life … and offers a secure retreat if we get beat up in the process.

Here's what we fail to consider: romantic love is only the tip of the iceberg. It's the initial flush, the first bloom, the shoot erupting from the soil that will one day become a flowering shrub filled with the most beautiful blooms. Just as in all gardens, the shrub might survive and even grace us with a few blooms if we ignore it, but to make it truly shine, we must invest time, effort, and money to bring it to its best. If the only effort we invest is to smell the blooms, we've missed out on something very special.

God desires to cultivate a deeper, more committed love with his children. His love is the one that never ends. We can depend on him.

The Eternal Covenant

The God of peace, who [gifted us] the blood
of the eternal covenant ...

— Hebrews 13:20 —

Eternal ... let's look at that word. The *Oxford Dictionary* tells us that something eternal lasts (or exists) forever. Then it goes further and says it has no beginning or ending.

When we apply this meaning to ideas and concepts, they become valid for all time, meaning they never change from the beginning to the end. How they started out is the same as they are now, and we can trust them to be the same in the future.

Now let's turn our attention to the word covenant. In its purest form, it means to strike up a contract. Both parties must agree and participate to bring about a mutual resolution. Did you get that? Both parties have an obligation *and responsibility* to do their part to maintain the covenant. If I love you but you no longer love me ... you can see where this goes. The covenant collapses, and it's no longer eternal.

That's what's special about our covenant with God. He is eternal. He has no beginning or end, and he never changes. He loved us before time, he loves us now, and he will continue to love us in the future. He will not *and cannot* fail to perform his end of the contract. In the Bible, we learn of five covenants God established with humanity. Let's see how they played out.

The first covenant was with Noah and is known as the Noahic Covenant. God flooded the land, and afterwards, he promised to never again sweep the land clean by means of a world-encompassing flood (Gen. 9:11). The rainbow is God's sign that he will always keep this covenant.

The Abrahamic Covenant was with Abraham who felt his bloodline ended with him. God declared otherwise, and God's covenant with Abraham included descendants, land (modern-day Israel), and a sweeping assurance of blessings upon each generation (Gen. 15; 17; 22). This covenant was marked by the circumcision of all males born in the bloodline of Abraham.

Under the Mosaic Covenant, Moses led the

Israelites from slavery in Egypt, and God's covenant was expressed through the commandments given to Moses on Mt. Sinai (Exodus 19-24). This covenant was marked (or maintained) by obedience to the Law as expressed in the Ten Commandments.

The Davidic Covenant, God's covenant with David, guaranteed that his descendants would reign on the throne forever (2 Sam. 7:8-11) and was marked/fulfilled through Jesus, who is the ultimate king.

Today, we are under the New Covenant. This contract with God is established through Jesus and guarantees forgiveness of sin and a new and intimate relationship with God. Rather than living underneath the Law as disseminated by the religious leadership, God writes his law on the hearts of his children (Jer. 31:31-34). When we accept the salvation offered by Jesus, we are changed from the person we once were into a new creation (2 Cor. 5:17).

Now let's return to our previous statement. *Both parties have an obligation and responsibility to do their part to maintain the covenant.* Our covenant is salvation and an eternal relationship with God. As an eternal being that is unchanging, God's love for us is forever established and always available to us. Our part is to accept his salvation plan, which means to realize that we have sinned; to put aside our old life and poor choices; and to model our future lifestyle after the example Jesus lived out for us. It's the old "what would Jesus do" question we must ask in every choice, decision, and circumstance we face.

God never divorces those who love him. We are his and he is ours—forever and amen.

Prepared for Perfect Love

My Father's house has many rooms ...

— John 14:2 —

It's not unusual to see church signs emblazoned as "The Father's House" or the "The Potter's House," and we call our churches "The House of God." In a sense, each church we discover as we wander through big cities or drive along country lanes is one small portion of the larger "house of God." Like a family with multiple children, each child's "room" might be differently decorated, host a variety of distinct friends, and receive varying levels of attention; but they all belong to the same family. God's perfect and eternal love flows into each "room" belonging to his family. One room might reflect a love for music, and another might be filled with books. Yet another might be empty much of the time, with its occupant out making connections throughout the city, reflecting a focus on missionary work.

None gain extra favor from God, for he loves them equally, often indulges them with special gifts, and occasionally must resort to finger wagging when things are let go for too long.

Yet, this verse is rarely equated with our earthly existence. Rather, we see it as the inexhaustible bounty available to us once we step through death's door to meet the Master. The truth is that the two are inextricably connected. Let's look at how God's path leads us from life on earth to eternity with him.

It all begins with the moment of Creation. God speaks, and we come into being. By creating us in his image, he endows us with his inherent value and dignity.

The gift of salvation through Jesus' death on the cross reveals the depths of his love for us. With this act, God establishes his commitment to our redemption and well-being.

His grace and mercy when we stumble are his reminder of his love toward us. Even in our darkest moments, he extends his grace and mercy, offering forgiveness and a chance to return to him.

He provides daily guidance through the presence of the Holy Spirit, the written expression of his Word, and divine encounters that we sometimes call coincidence. God uses each of these to show his comfort, offer encouragement, and bestow upon us his wisdom. He gifts us his unwavering support each day.

God also disciplines us, but he balances it with restoration. He loves us even when we make mistakes, and he desires to surround us with his unwavering and eternal love. He will correct us when we make mistakes, but he draws us close with forgiveness and restoration. What is stripped from us is put back together by his hand of mercy.

And through all this, as John 14:2 suggests, God is preparing our heavenly home for us. What will it look like? Streets of gold, surely. What will be in the many "rooms" we find there? Eternal life, that's the big one. It's a central premise of the New Testament and Christ's salvation message to his followers. We will have forever to worship the Father and commune with one another.

A big bonus is that sorrow will be vanquished. No more tears. Only joy will be allowed to enter the heavenly gates, for our sense of awe and abandonment for the beauty of our God will overshadow every other emotion. On the other side of those gates, we will discover a perfect community of believers, all of one accord and filled with love and truth. Each person we interact with will be focused on the glory of the Father, the love of the Son, and the connectivity of the Holy Spirit. We will be as one in heart and intent.

More concisely, there will be no tears (Rev. 7:17); no separation (Rev. 21:1); no sorrow or death (Rev. 21:4); no morning or night (Rev. 21:25); no sin (Rev. 21:27); and no more curse (Rev. 23:3a). We will discover The Throne of God and of the Lamb where his servants (that's us) will serve him for all eternity (Rev. 23:3b)!

The KJV says it like this: *In my Father's house are many mansions ...* How glorious that day will be!

Face to Face with Love Himself

When Christ appears, we shall be like
Him ...

— I John 3:2 —

A personal encounter with Jesus changes us forever. We have multiple examples in the Bible, and each reveals something of the love of Our Lord for his creation.

Let's look first at the Samaritan woman at the well. She went from being a social outcast to a powerful evangelist. She ran back into town to share her encounter with Jesus with her family and community, and she led many to Jesus. Her concept of herself changed from ignorance to knowledge, shame to hope, doubt to conviction, and from a consuming self-centered focus on her needs to an outward reach that invited others to share her transformation.

Next let's talk about the Canaanite woman with the sick daughter. Her persistent plea for the help of Jesus seemed to be ignored by him. What?!? Jesus *ignored* a request for healing? Yes, until the woman humbled herself and admitted she didn't deserve Jesus' attention. She broke the barrier between the Jews and the gentiles, leading to her daughter's healing and Jesus including the gentiles in his message of love and salvation.

The Roman Centurion is a bit of an outlier. His servant was ill, and he desired him to receive healing from Jesus. He came with a deep faith, saying, "If only you say the word." Here, Jesus acknowledges that the Centurion's faith—someone who was not a Jew—is greater than that in all of Israel. The healing power of Jesus only deepened the man's faith and convinced him that Jesus was not only a healer but truly divine (Matt. 27:54).

Mary Magdalene was the first to encounter the resurrected Christ (Mk. 16:9-10; Jn. 20:14-17). This was a woman who had already received physical and spiritual healing from Jesus and had become a devoted follower. She was present at his crucifixion and now, she is instructed to share the news of his resurrection with the disciples. Through her connection to Jesus, she plays a vital part in establishing Christianity and revealing the importance of resiliency in faith.

Of course, our story is incomplete without the

story of Paul's face-to-face meeting with Jesus. He was on the road to Damascus, on his way to terrorize yet another group of believers, when he was struck down and blinded. In that encounter, Paul (Saul at the time) shifted his focus entirely and changed from Christ-beater to Christ-believer and is today one of the foundation stones of modern Christianity and the author of many of the most beloved books of the New Testament.

What do face-to-face encounters with Jesus look like today? Some people experience his power and grace through vivid images in their mind. Others dream of him or have what the Bible calls a vision. The love of Jesus might be felt while in nature viewing a dramatic waterfall or a towering mountain. We feel "connected" to him and enjoy a surge of faith, hope, and comfort. Others say a near-death encounter has changed how they view Jesus. In that moment of uncertainty, they develop a connection with him like never before.

One thing is certain. When we come face-to-face with Jesus, we are different when we step away. We can choose to let our meeting devolve into an interesting story, one filled with emotion and truth, but essentially a byline in our life; or we can choose to step closer to him, let him lead us to a new degree of commitment to God, and let our actions reflect that age-old question, "In the circumstance in which I find myself, if Jesus were here, what would he do?"

Jesus would do only that which leaves behind a sense of love, peace, and joy. Any other action means we never really understood who he really is.

No More Pain, Only Love

He will wipe every tear from their eyes ...

— Revelation 21:4 —

The human condition is something we've come to recognize as endemic to life, no matter how upbeat or lucky we might be. People come into our lives, and then they move on to pursue new goals or enjoy different vistas. We embrace good health when we are young, but then time takes a toll on our joints, ears, and eyes. The new home we purchase to live in forever becomes tired and dated. Our car forms rust, the seats begin to wear, then it refuses to start at the worst possible time.

Pain is woven into the human condition. It encourages us to walk carefully to bypass the most dangerous spots. We bump a cupboard, and the sharp sensation reminds us to be more vigilant. We over-share with gossipers, and the hateful pushback tells us, "Never again."

The Bible never says that in this life things will be perfect, yet in Isaiah 41:10 we read: "I will strengthen you, I will help you, I will uphold you with my righteous right hand." Isaiah 43:2 says it like this: "When you pass through the waters, I will be with you; and when you pass through the rivers, they will not sweep over you. When you walk through the fire, you will not be burned; the flames will not set you ablaze."

So, what does our verse in Revelation mean? How can God wipe every tear from our eyes if he doesn't remove the pain?

First, he offers us comfort and peace. He holds out his hand to the brokenhearted and those crushed in spirit (Ps. 34:18) and provides a peace that "passes understanding." He guards both hearts and minds (Phil. 4:7).

Second, God strengthens and empowers us when we are weak. His grace is sufficient for us to endure any hardship (2 Cor. 12:9), and through him, we will learn to overcome challenges, develop perseverance, and become more like Jesus.

Third, he reveals his truth and purpose through his Word. By means of his love and mercy, he guides us down a path to a closer walk with him. When we do face suffering, he gently reveals his character to us through his promise to be with us through it all.

Fourth, when trials test our faith, we can sense his guiding hand in the patience, forgiveness, and compassion that grows in us. He brings out in us new levels of empathy, humility, and understanding for what others might be going through. We learn to see God's hand in our pain and develop trust that he is working out our situation for our good.

Fifth, we find hope for the future revealed through the divine and enduring love of God. We can look past our pain because we understand that he is working all things for our good (Rom. 8:28); that suffering is temporary and he will be with us through it (Rev. 21:4); and that there is a future coming when there will be no more suffering, and we will live in his presence forever (Ps. 23:6).

God will wipe every tear from our eyes, repeatedly in this world and permanently in the world to come. Because we are human and alive, we remain immersed in the human condition, but we are not abandoned to it. God desires to hold us close, guide us daily, and create a space that is safe for us to relax and trust in him.

Trust. It's the game-changer. The wind can blow, the storms can batter the walls, and the waters can rise; but when we learn to place our hope in Jesus, all of it is of no consequence. We know he has it all under his control. We are wrapped in his love, and his touch is a balm that soothes every pain that life brings.

Forever Held, Forever Known

I will dwell in the house of the Lord forever.

— Psalm 23:6 —

The secular world says we live and we die, with only the years indicated by the dash between our birth and our death to claim as our own. How can forever apply to humanity?

This verse in Psalms says that we will live in the house of the Lord forever. How can we know for sure? Our confidence comes from placing our faith in Jesus and confessing him as Lord. As Romans 10:9 says, "If you declare with your mouth, 'Jesus is Lord,' and believe in your heart that God raised him from the dead, you will be saved."

Let's unpack that verse. First comes our faith in Jesus. We must believe on him and recognize him as the Son of God and that he died for our sins. Next we must confess him as Lord with an outward expression of our faith in him. We must acknowledge him publicly as our savior and authority in life.

A central tenet of our Christian faith is our belief in his resurrection. It's what Easter is all about, rather than the rabbits and eggs that children find so fascinating. Our risen Lord gives us hope for our own resurrection into eternal life. We see this in John 3:16 with the promise, "For God so loved the world, that he gave his only Son, that whoever believes in him should not perish but have eternal life."

When we claim salvation through the death and resurrection of Jesus, we will begin to live differently, a life transformed. We will reflect our faith in Christ, and the world will see it through our repentance of our wrongdoing, through the forgiveness we both receive and offer unto others, and the love of God that we feel for everyone around us.

Our assurance is further strengthened by our hope of reuniting with loved ones who have gone on before us. John 14:1-3 says: "Do not let your hearts be troubled. You believe in God; believe also in me. My Father's house has many rooms; if that were not so, would I have told you that I am going there to prepare a place for you? And if I go and prepare a place for you, I will come back and take you to be with me that you also may be where I am."

Some say that heaven is our goal. That's true, but it's like saying that going on a vacation is only about the end point. What's between here and there is of no importance. Yet many of our best memories come from what takes place between here and there. Some years ago, my family took an overnight drive to visit relatives in Colorado Springs. We expected to arrive just after breakfast to have the entire day to visit but made better time than expected and were early. Wasted time, right? No! We diverted through the city and were pleasantly surprised to discover a huge hot air balloon festival, with dozens of massive, deflated balloons strewn throughout the city park. We were able to stop, walk among the balloons, talk to the people preparing them to launch, and watch as they filled and rose lazily into the sky. If we had bypassed the city and headed straight to our destination, we would have had hours to kill and missed out on one of the most special memories we hold.

Forever held, forever known. When we place our trust in Jesus, there's no place we can go that we are not under his protecting love. In this life and in the life beyond, when our path takes us a different direction and we must change our plans, when what we actually do comes from necessity rather than from dreams, we can trust that God knows what he's doing, and our faith in him will grow strong and sure, for he loves with a passion that is unbreakable and will never fail.

You've finished *God's Love!*

Congratulations!

I sincerely hope God blesses you with his love across every season of your life. I want you to feel forever held and forever known by the Great I Am, our adoring Father God, through whom we live, breathe, and have our existence.

Amen.